HOW TO UNLOCK THE SECRETS OF LOVE, SEX AND MARRIAGE

Rusty Wright
and
Linda Raney Wright

BARBOUR BOOKS
164 Mill Street
Westwood, New Jersey 07675

ACKNOWLEDGMENTS

We want to express our gratitude to everyone who provided encouragement and ideas in the preparation of this book. We cannot mention everyone by name, but we want to express special thanks to Josh McDowell, whose life and work in this area have inspired us both. His popular lectures on love and sex have offered both motivation and insight for this project, and his friendship is something that we value greatly.

We are also grateful to the many students, faculty, and lay-persons across the nation whose questions have challenged our thinking as we have lectured on this topic. They have prompted us to continually improve our material!

Rusty Wright
Linda Raney Wright

WHAT OTHERS SAY ABOUT THIS BOOK

". . . an exciting new book on a subject which is of great interest to most people—adolescents to senior citizens. Chapter 6 in particular, 'Getting the Most Out of Sex,' is 'must' reading for anyone interested in building truly satisfying intimate relationships."

James C. Coleman, Ph.D.
Professor of Psychology, UCLA
Author of the university
textbooks *Contemporary Psychology
and Effective Behavior* and *Abnormal
Psychology and Modern Life*

"Rusty and Linda Wright have marshalled reliable scientific and sociologic evidence to document a healthy perspective on human sexuality. . . . This book should be read by all who seek truth."

William P. Wilson, M.D.
Professor of Psychiatry
Duke University Medical Center

"In highly readable fashion, this book lays a solid foundation for the best sexual adjustments in marriage. As a family physician and marriage counselor, I recommend it heartily."

Ed Wheat, M.D.
Certified Sex Therapist
Author of *Intended for Pleasure*

OTHER BOOKS

By Rusty Wright and Linda Raney Wright—
    Dynamic Sex

By Linda Raney Wright—
    Raising Children
    Success Helper

By Rusty Wright—
    The Other Side of Life

ABOUT THE AUTHORS

Rusty Wright is an author and traveling speaker. He was born in Miami, Florida, and was educated at the Choate School, Wallingford, Connecticut. He has a bachelor of science degree in psychology from Duke University and a master of arts degree from the International School of Theology. A popular speaker, he lectures each year to thousands of students, faculty, and laypersons in major universities and cities across the nation. He has spoken on over 120 campuses in the United States, Canada, and Europe and has also lectured in Asia. He is a member of two national honor societies. His articles have appeared in numerous periodicals and he has authored a book on out-of-body experiences, *The Other Side of Life*.

Linda Raney Wright was born in San Diego, California, and has an A.B. degree in rhetoric from University of California at Berkeley. In addition to lecturing on various campuses and in cities across the United States, she is an accomplished writer. Her articles have appeared in *Ladies' Home Journal, Decision,* and many other magazines and newspapers. Her first book, *Raising Children,* a collection of interviews with famous women, was released by Tyndale House in 1975. *Success Helper* (Tyndale House) was published in 1980. Linda was featured as one of 20 leading women in the recent book *Why Doesn't Somebody Do Something?* by Daisy Hepburn (Victor, 1980).

The Wrights are frequent guests on television talk shows in cities around the nation.

To:
Mike and Joyce Hopping

FOREWORD

Almost everyone is interested in love and sex. Years of speaking and counseling with men and women around the globe have shown me the need for reliable guidance in this sensitive area.

Amid the myriad of current literature on this topic are certain important foundational principles which are sometimes overlooked. This book presents some of these principles. When properly applied, they can add new dimension to anyone's love life.

Rusty and Linda Wright have been good friends of mine for a number of years. Together they write from a wide background of speaking and counseling with students, faculty, and laypersons in universities and cities across the continent. Their insight into relationships will be obvious to anyone who reads this book.

This is not a book about technique. Rather, it offers a fresh perspective on the principles, attitudes, and relationships that form the basis of a fulfilling love and sex life. It is clearly and logically written. Witty at times and serious at others, it should appeal to a wide spectrum of readers—young and old, married and single. I think you will find it as enjoyable as my wife Dottie and I did when we read it. I am happy to recommend it.

Josh McDowell
Author and Lecturer

CONTENTS

CHAPTER ONE

A GREAT LOVE LIFE

"A fulfilling love life—how can I have one?"

Men and women across the country are asking questions like this. Married couples, singles, high school students, university students, even older adults share this concern. We know because we've talked with many of these people in our travels. We've found that people everywhere want to know how to have the most fulfilling love lives possible. They want to know how to unlock the secrets of successful love, sex, and marriage.

There are a few simple principles which, if understood and applied correctly, can help to produce a fulfilling love life. These principles aren't as widely understood as you might think. "You told me some things I had never heard," said a student in Michigan. "I'll probably remember these things the rest of my life," remarked a man in Kansas. "I brought the woman I'm dating tonight to hear you speak," explained a young man in California after one of our lectures; "I'm sure this will help our relationship." One of our all-time favorite comments came from a woman on the West Coast: "Thank you. I enjoyed your lecture—to my amazement. I am a great-grandmother!"

Today there is a great quantity of instruction on love, sex, and marriage available on the market. Much of it is good because it has bred a certain wholesome openness as well as offered guidelines and techniques. But is there more to be said on the subject?

We believe so. Naturally we are not claiming that we have all the answers or the perfect relationship! Any lasting, intimate bond involves a growing process between two imperfect people. Of course, like any couple, we have a lot to learn. Nevertheless, there are several qualities that we have found beneficial and which thousands of other couples and many professional counselors agree are important. It is in this spirit and context that we present some suggestions.

To the satisfied customer who may not realize that there is something better; to the individual who may have read widely on the topic but is still asking, "Is that all there is?"; and to the person who is just plain curious: to you we dedicate this book.

Do you want to have a good love life? Then this is not the book for you.

Do you want to have a *great* love life? Then read on!

CHAPTER TWO

ALL YOU NEED IS LOVE

We first met when Linda had a date with one of my (Rusty's) roommates. It was September of 1973 and we both lived in Atlanta, Georgia. I didn't really think about her very much until about four months later, when I ended up giving her a ride from Atlanta to Auburn, Alabama. I was going to speak at a meeting and she wanted to visit a friend of hers.

On the way down we talked about lots of things. She told me about places she had been and people she had met as she traveled around the country getting interviews for her first book. I was fascinated with her, and the 2½-hour trip went by quickly.

When we got to Auburn, I spoke at the meeting, Linda visited with her friend, and we headed home. The return trip took about three hours. I drove a bit slower, since I was enjoying her company so much!

We had found an unusual openness in our conversation in the car, and Linda began to share with me some of her thoughts on marriage. She had just been through a romantic disappointment, so the subject was on her mind.

I could see from our conversation that Linda wanted to get married. I could also see that she was not desperately chasing men. Rather, she was determined to wait for just the right person. When I let her off at her apartment that evening, I said, "Linda, I'm going to pray that you find a husband real soon." Little did I know that, several months later, I would become the answer to that prayer!

As we began to spend time together, we began to learn lots of lessons about love. (We're still learning new ones, and sometimes relearning the old ones, too!) We saw what it meant to be in love, and we developed practical ways to communicate our love to each other. Today as we travel, speak, and counsel, we find that many people have questions about this area. They wonder, "What *is* love?" "What does it mean to say 'I love you'?" and "How can I show my partner that I love him or her?"

Perspectives on Love

A philosopher has defined love as a "feeling you feel you're going to feel when you have a feeling you feel you haven't felt before!" Maybe you can identify with that.

Dr. Karl Meninger states, "Love is the medicine for the sickness of the world." He has informed his staff—doctors, nurses, orderlies, and maintenance workers—that the most important thing they can offer any patient is love. He says that *if people can learn to give and receive love,* they will recover from their physical or emotional illnesses. And, viewing the situation in much the same way, a growing number of doctors trace psychic, emotional and physical disorders to a loveless condition in life.[1]

The Greek language has several different words for love. *Eros* means a sexual or passionate love. Our word "erotic" conveys a similar meaning. *Phileo* means a tender affection, a very high type of friendship or brotherly love. Philadelphia, which comes from the word *phileo,* is called the city of brotherly love. *Agape* (ah-GAH-pay) refers to the highest kind of love, a self-giving, unconditional type. *Agape* loves another person not because of what that person does, but *in spite of it.*

---

[1] All numbered notes are listed at the back of this book.

There is nothing wrong with any of these types of love in themselves. In fact, each is needed for a maximum relationship. Ideally, partners will "eros" each other—they'll turn each other on. They'll also "phileo" each other—consider themselves best friends. And they'll also attempt to "agape"—give to and care for each other unconditionally.

I Love You

In order to better understand the type of love that is essential for a strong personal relationship, consider several other meanings of those romantic words "I love you." In his popular movie *The Secret of Loving*, Josh McDowell illustrates three variations. One meaning is "I love you *if*—if you do what I like, if you are lighthearted, if you sleep with me." This type of love attaches requirements to love. Love is given *if* the other person performs well. It says, "You must *do* something to earn my love."

Another meaning is "I love you *because*—because you are attractive, because you are strong, because you are intelligent. This type of love is given on the basis of what a person *is*. It says that you must *be* something to earn my love. Both types of love must be *earned*.

There is nothing wrong with wanting to be loved for what you are, but problems can arise with having *if* or *because of* love as the basis of a relationship. Jealousy can set in when someone who is more attractive or more intelligent appears and the partner's affection shifts to the newcomer. People who know they are loved only for their strong points may be afraid to admit any weaknesses to their partners. The relationship becomes rigid and less than honest.

The best kind of love is unconditional. It doesn't say, "I love you if." It doesn't say, "I love you because." It says, "I love you, *period*. I love you even if someone better looking comes along, even with your faults, and even if you change. I want to give myself to you. I place your needs above my own." *Agape* love is based on the character of the one loving rather than on the character of the one being loved; it is based on his or her ability to love rather than the "lovability" of the partner.

Unconditional Love

Psychiatrist Elisabeth Kubler-Ross asks, "Do we love people as long as they can give us something in return? When they fix our meals and take care of our laundry . . . ? That is not love as far as I'm concerned."[2] Real unconditional love seeks another person's best interests, seeks to give even when nothing is given in return. Of course, we're not advocating need-denial. We all have needs for love, acceptance, pleasure, etc., and it is important that we be aware of those needs and have them met. But a paradox of life is that we receive love by giving love. If one partner in a relationship initiates unselfish love, most often the other partner will respond in kind. There must be a balance—not a 50-percent-to-50-percent balance, but a 100-percent-to-100-percent balance.

Bedrooms and Deodorant

Consider a very simple illustration of *agape* love, as Linda tells it.

Shortly after we were married, Rusty learned that I was allergic to aerosol sprays. He found this out on our honeymoon when I told him, "Your spray deodorant is killing me!" He had used spray deodorant for years and wasn't about to switch, so he tried some alternatives. First he tried closing the bathroom door, but I claimed that the fumes crept under the door into the bedroom. (And you know, they did!) Putting a towel under the door didn't help either—some of the fumes always escaped when he left the bathroom. We travel and stay in motels a lot, and Rusty envisioned what might happen. "I could get up very early," he reasoned, "and sneak outside to put on my deodorant while no one was looking." But we travel in the winter and it gets pretty cold outside! Finally he decided that it was better to switch than fight, so he changed to stick deodorant. *Agape* love in action!

Rusty continues with a more serious example.

This one occurred before we were married. We had agreed on a certain wedding date. Though we both knew of some specific potential problems with that date, I firmly insisted that I would not change my mind after we had set it. The invitations were printed and the wedding arrangements were made.

Then, due to some circumstances in my own life, I changed my mind and wanted to postpone the wedding. After much deliberation, we agreed that the next possible date was almost a year later.

Some of you women may think that I had given due cause for justifiable homicide! It was a difficult time for Linda and a definite challenge to our relationship. Yet, instead of terminating our engagement or belittling me for my indecision, she graciously forgave me, demonstrating her unconditional love for me.

Some Probing Questions

Though none of us is perfect, we can have unconditional love with respect to many specific situations, and the overall pattern of our love can become *less* conditional. Here's a question for you to ponder: the last time you kissed your date or partner or spouse, was it to please the other person or to please yourself? Have you ever heard this one—"If you love me, you'd let me?" Anyone who persists when you say no is not saying "I love you." He is saying, "I *love me* and I *want you*." Real love is tender and prompts people to deny themselves for those whom they love.

One young couple had a beautiful romance. They had similar interests and were extremely popular and strikingly attractive. Then the young woman had a skiing accident that left her paralyzed for life. (Her story was portrayed in the popular film "The Other Side of the Mountain.") Her fiance deserted her. He couldn't go through with it. Did he love her *period*? Or was it "I love you if" or "I love you because"? Of course this was a complex situation, and some may argue the implications. Still, it forces us all to rethink our own attitudes about love. Think of the person with whom you may now be romantically involved. If his (her) face or body were disfigured in an auto accident, would you have the capacity to love him (her) just as much? Your thoughts on this may help you to evaluate the quality of love in your relationship. (We'll discuss more about *agape* love in a later chapter.)

Self-Esteem

One of the most important reasons that love is so necessary for a successful relationship is that *it helps build self-esteem in both partners.* If you know you are loved, you tend to feel good about yourself. This in turn can motivate you to demonstrate love in return.

Let's suppose that one morning the telephone rings and a neighbor of yours is on the line. This neighbor says, "I'm sure glad I caught you before you left for the morning. I've just been thinking about what an outstanding person you are, and I wanted to tell you how I felt. You are always so positive, so thoughtful, so kind. Just being around you motivates me to be a better person! I'm proud to have you as a neighbor and friend!"

Then let's say you drive to a nearby store, one at which you regularly shop, and you pick up a few items. While you're standing in line to pay for your merchandise, the manager of the store comes up to you, greets you by name, and speaks to you so that everyone nearby can hear. "I just want you to know how pleased we are to have you as our customer," he says. "You are always so congenial, so friendly, so patient in the checkout lines! Our cashiers tell me they can always tell when you've come into the store by the way things seem to brighten up. Your sparkle is contagious."

Or suppose you go to your place of work just in time for that regular employees' meeting. Your boss is there, and just after you take your seat he begins the meeting. "Before we consider our usual business," he announces, "I want to take a moment to recognize one of our most outstanding employees." (He recognizes you by name.) "I want everyone in this company to know what a fine worker this person is. He is always on time, never complains about extra work, and even seeks out opportunities to improve our company. Your cheerful attitude is commendable. In the 25 years I've been with this outfit I've seen many employees come and go, but never have I seen someone with such integrity, such proficiency, and such enthusiasm."

Thank you for being a part of our company."[3]

After you recover from your daydream about these encounters, we would like to ask you a question: wouldn't those encounters make you feel good about yourself? You would think, "Wow! I must be something special! My neighbor, that store manager, and my boss all think so, and they're no dummies!" Wouldn't you be especially motivated to be a better neighbor, a better customer, and a better employee? Probably you would. Their love and kindness toward you would have enhanced your self-esteem and would prompt you to demonstrate kindness to them. The same holds true in a relationship with your spouse or date, as we will see a bit later.

The night before our wedding, Rusty's dad took him aside to offer a bit of fatherly advice. We had just finished the rehearsal dinner with family and friends in the wedding party. This was to be the last time that Rusty and his father would have by themselves before the wedding, the next afternoon. One of his remarks related to the importance of unconditional love. "Always remember, son," he said, "that the time you may think Linda deserves love the *least* is the time she needs it the *most*."

CHAPTER THREE

HOW DO I LOVE YOU?

"How do I love you? Let me count the ways."

Love given most often prompts love in return. The same principle holds true in a romantic relationship. If you take the initiative to demonstrate love, more than likely you will receive it back in return.

There are several practical ways to demonstrate love. We would like to mention four: compliments, courtesy, giving, and creativity.

Compliments

An ancient proverb says, "Anxiety in the heart of a man weighs it down, but a good word makes it glad."[1]

Mark Twain said, "I can live off one good compliment a week."[2] An old Japanese saying affirms, "One kind word can warm three winter months."[3]

We all appreciate well-placed compliments. They can do wonders for our state of mind! Bob, a friend of ours, had lunch one afternoon at a fast-food restaurant in Miami. He noticed that the young woman who was making his ham sandwich seemed quite shy and forlorn. She was small and not very attractive, and her face was scarred with acne. She looked as if she wanted to hide from the world as she slouched over her work station. Bob ate the sandwich and went on his way.

Because his schedule that day was rather full, Bob found that he had only a short time in which to eat dinner. So he returned to the same fast-food restaurant that evening. As he stood at the counter, he could see that the young woman who had made his sandwich was still working. He told the cashier he wanted to speak to the manager.

Bob is quite an imposing figure—he played center for the University of Miami football team and stands six feet four inches and weighs 225 pounds! When he asked to see the manager, the cashier and the forlorn sandwich maker both winced. They remembered him as having eaten lunch there and must have expected the worst. "You w-w-want to s-s-see the m-m-manager?" asked the frightened cashier." "Yes, that's right," answered Bob.

When the manager came, Bob introduced himself and told him, "I ate lunch here this afternoon and had one of your ham sandwiches. I wonder if you might tell me who it is that makes your ham sandwiches." The young, forlorn sandwich maker, who could easily hear the conversation, looked more forlorn than ever. She looked as if she wanted to melt away, vanish into thin air, commit hara-kiri, or all of the above.

The manager replied, "Why, this young woman over here makes them," and he motioned to the sandwich maker. "Well, sir," Bob continued, "I just wanted you to know that of all the ham sandwiches I have ever eaten, that one I had for lunch today was definitely the most outstanding. In fact it was so good that I have come back to have another one for dinner. I wanted you to know that I feel that you and your employees are doing a fine job and that you serve *great* ham sandwiches!"

If human beings could float like balloons, they would have had to pull that young woman down from the ceiling. She stood straight up, and the smile that came across her face put the Cheshire Cat to shame!

We all appreciate compliments. They can pick us up when we are down or show us that someone thinks we are special. Try to think of genuine compliments you can make to your spouse or friend—not vain flattery that is only designed to ultimately gain attention for yourself, but sincere appreciation of genuine attributes or actions. Tell him (her) how much you appreciate his sense of humor, how attractive or handsome he looks, or how much you appreciate his yardwork, housecleaning, or cooking.

One young husband found a clever way of communicating to his wife which meals he liked best. He didn't want to negatively criticize her for meals he wasn't too fond of, so he decided to give extra praise for meals that he especially liked. His wife began to get the picture, and they both enjoyed dinnertime even more.

Try sprinkling a few compliments into your daily conversation. Be careful not to overdo it, though, or you'll come across as a phony. Use compliments thoughtfully and watch your relationship begin to sparkle. Compliments can help demonstrate your love.

Courtesy

Common courtesies are still in vogue. Words like "please" and "thank you" sometimes tend to get lost as familiarity grows, but almost everyone appreciates them. They help you to avoid one of the most deadly sins in a relationship: taking the other person for granted.

Simple pointers like opening a door for someone else, being on time, and phoning if you have to be late will work as well with your mate as they do with your friends or business associates. If your spouse or friend wants to talk or wants to be left alone, try to respect his desire. This seems hardest at the times when your desires don't coincide with his. You want to talk but he wants privacy, or he wants to talk but you want to be left alone. Of course there will be times when you each have to bend. Chances are, though, that the more you take the initiative to be courteous, the more courtesy you'll get in return. Courtesy helps to demonstrate your love.

Giving

One of the most successful bits of advice we've ever heard for successful relationships came from an ancient writer. He was writing about human relationships in general, but his words apply to romantic relationships as well. He said, "Be devoted to one another in . . . love, give preference to one another in honor."[4] In other words, he was saying, *"Outdo* one another in showing concern." We're not saying that you have to always deny your needs. But a relationship can really grow and develop if each person is concerned about the other. Ask yourself, "What can I give in this relationship?" instead of just "What can I get?" It can help relieve pressure and help you enjoy each other more.

Helping with chores is one tangible way to give. In our home Linda usually does the cooking and Rusty washes the dishes. We each consider it a special treat when, without being asked, Rusty prepares a meal or Linda does the dishes.

Giving gifts is another way to express love. Birthdays and holidays aren't the only occasions for this, either. When returning home from a trip, when celebrating a certain success, or really *any time at all* are good occasions for gifts. And they don't have to be expensive—a bunch of flowers, a coffee mug from some faraway place, some candles or bath oil beads. The fact that you're giving the gift is what's most important. It says "I care about you," "I missed you," or "I just want you to know I'm thinking about you."

Linda has several coffee mugs from around the nation—gifts from Rusty. One time she surprised him by wallpapering his study and putting up shelves. Linda has a special nickname for Rusty, one of those cuddly, tender, affectionate nicknames that a husband and wife share only between themselves. The initials of this nickname are "TGBB." Once Linda surprised Rusty with a specially made coffee mug that had the initials "TGBB" on the side. Two of her closest women friends are just dying to know what "TGBB" stands for, but she'll *never* tell them! (No, we're not going to tell you either!)

Creativity

There are lots of creative things that couples can do together. Creativity helps to express love. Don't always get tied down to the same old routine. Activities that couples are involved in usually fall into two categories—things you do as *spectators* and things you do as *participants*. Spectator activities are things you both observe together, such as sporting events, television, etc. These can be fun, but they can also become routine, especially if they keep you from communicating. That's why it's good to plan activities that you can both be involved in together. For example, go out to a restaurant, splurge on a deluxe hamburger, and then talk for a couple of hours. (Just be sure you have an understanding waitress!)

When we were first dating, Linda used to work with some underprivileged kids that lived near her home. We did all kinds of things together with them. We played baseball, went on picnics, and acted out stories. One time we even borrowed a bus, packed it full of kids, and took them all to the circus. Not only did the kids have a good time, but Linda and I got to know each other better as we saw each other in many different types of situations. We've tried to carry this participation theme over into our marriage, too. Whether it's riding mopeds together, going on family outings, or reading a special book together, we try to add creativity to our romance.

There are all kinds of sports you can be involved in together—bowling, tennis, ping-pong, skating, miniature golf, snow skiing, waterskiing, hiking, surfing, softball, swimming, and jogging.

Sometimes single people come up with more creative ideas than married folks do, and the marrieds might take note. At the University of Arizona, one young man told his steady date that they would go out "real fancy" for a special evening. He drove her all around town and then brought her back to the mall in the center of campus. He had arranged for some friends of his to set up a table for two—candles and all—and cater a formal dinner for the two of them on the middle tier of the steps right in the center of campus! People would walk by, going up and down the steps, and stare as the two of them ate by candlelight. It was a date they never forgot!

You say you cannot envision you and your partner dining like that in the middle of Times Square? Maybe something more subdued, but just as much fun, would be in order. How about an invitation to lunch when they least expect it, breakfast in bed, a surprise birthday party, or _____ (you fill in the blank!). The fact that you took the time to do something special says to your partner, "I think you are special." Creativity helps you to demonstrate love.

CHAPTER FOUR

I'M IN LOVE!

I (Rusty) first got to know Linda while driving to Auburn, Alabama. That next week I couldn't seem to get her off my mind. I didn't really think much about love, but just about what an interesting person she was. We began to see each other and we did all kinds of things together. We went on picnics, went to the beach at a local lake, and went to basketball games. And, as mentioned earlier, I helped her organize activities for some young children.

One evening we were having dinner at a pizza place. I was having my favorite—a medium mushroom and black olive pizza, thin-'n-crispy. We began to casually broach the subject of love. We were not really talking about *ourselves*, you understand. Rather, we were talking in sort of academic terms about how a person could know whether he or she is in love. (We probably both knew that the "academic" tone of our conversation helped us ease into the topic with a minimum of risk!) I had always heard people say, "You'll just *know* when you're in love," but I told her that this had never made much sense to me.

Hedging My Bets

As time went on I sensed that my affection for Linda was

growing. She likes to tell the story on me about another, less academic conversation we had in which I made a bold attempt to convey my intentions toward her.

We were on a picnic in Stone Mountain Park, near Atlanta. Rusty had been seeing me quite a bit and wanted to let me know that his feelings toward me were more than just casual. At the same time he wanted to find out how I felt about him. So he found the sneakiest way to do it.

"Linda," he began, clearing his throat a bit formally, "I know we have been seeing each other a lot and I suppose you have been wondering how I feel about you." For the next 15 minutes he rambled incessantly. What ultimately came across was that he felt we were just good friends. All the time he was speaking, he watched me intently for any clues to my feelings.

When Rusty finished, he said a bit sheepishly, "Um, Linda . . . um . . . are you disappointed?" I replied, "Well . . . maybe."

SHAZAM! That was all he needed! With renewed courage he announced that he thought he might even be in love with me and asked if we could continue the relationship to see if something might develop!

Pros and Cons

Still, though, Rusty's feelings were not completely clear.

I knew that I enjoyed being with her more than I could express, but I still needed to sort a few things out. Then one day Linda asked me how I made other decisions in life. That question hit me like a sledgehammer. I realized that, in other areas, I tried to use sound reasoning. In fact, I often made a list of the pros and cons and evaluated the alternatives.

Later that night, after I returned home, I began to make a list about our relationship. Now I do not mean to imply that it was all reason and no emotion. I was very emotionally attracted to her in the first place. But love is more than an emotion. It includes the emotions but it involves your total personality.

As I made my list, I tried to consider Linda as a total person. Here are some of the items I had on my list:

1. Intellectually, she was sharp as a tack. She was a graduate of the University of California at Berkeley, a

professional writer, and a deep and seasoned thinker. I had always done well academically, but I found myself being motivated by her example to be even more precise in my thinking, speaking, and writing. We had seen that we could complement each other in the intellectual area.

2. Emotionally, Linda was a woman of tremendous compassion. If someone had a need, she tried to meet it. She was so sensitive to others. The more time I spent around her, the more I found her sensitivity rubbing off on me. I was no Hitler to begin with, but I found myself becoming more and more sensitive toward people I worked with and people I met.

3. Physically . . . well, no problem there! I knew what I liked and I liked what I saw! I *knew* I was attracted to her in that area. She was built just the way I liked.

4. Socially and spiritually, I could see that we were both on the same wavelength and headed in the same direction.

5. We each wanted a teammate.

6. Our hearts were both captivated by the same cause.

7. The thought of spending the rest of my life with Linda seemed natural and good.

My final list had 26 pros and only one con. You probably wonder what the con was, don't you? It was just a vague fear that things would not work out. It was not really based on anything substantial, but was simply a vague fear of the unknown, like I used to get as a small child on the first day of school. Since I did not have a solid basis for this feeling, I decided not to let it sway me. Based on what I had seen, I concluded that this was true love and that we should get married.

Countdown

Still, though, there was this small matter of telling *Linda* how I felt. Several days went by. Then one Sunday afternoon we were together in her living room. I knew I had to tell her.

There she was, seated on the couch . . . on the left-hand side, and there I was, seated on the same couch . . . on the left-hand side! It was ten minutes till three in the afternoon.

I had never told Linda that I loved her before this. You see, by this time in my life I had had enough of infatuation and shallow romances. I wanted to be sure that if I ever said "I love you" I was willing to follow it with an all-out commitment.

I knew I had to tell her but I couldn't seem to get the words out! Then I decided to try something my dad had taught me. I decided to count to ten—silently—and when I reached ten, I would say to my mouth, "Mouth, speak!" I started to count: one . . . two . . . . three . . . . . four . . . . . . five . . . . six . . . . seven . . . . eight . . . . nine . . . . ten . . . . I chickened out!

Half an hour later, though, I counted to ten again. This time the words came out. "Linda," I said, "I love you very much and it would make me very happy if you would marry me." She said she felt the same way about me! Actually, we decided to put it to a vote, and it was unanimous!

Well, that is how Rusty knew he was in love.

Linda's method of knowing she was in love runs a little differently and more simply. "There was an intuitive 'rightness' about the relationship, a sense that I was right where I should be."

Am I Really in Love

Recently we received a letter from a young woman asking if we thought she should marry a certain man. Since we did not know either of them, we were hesitant to say anything definite. Instead, we suggested that she ask herself several questions. These questions may be helpful in your own situation, or maybe (if you are married) you will want to show them to a friend.

1. What are our mutual interests? Do we enjoy doing things together? If you are going to spend the rest of your lives with each other, you had better be sure you can have fun together.

2. Am I attracted to this person, to his or her total personality—intellectually, physically, emotionally, spiritually? Is he or she attracted to the total me?

3. Am I honest with myself about this person's faults? (To see someone as perfect can be a sign of infatuation rather than love.) Am I willing to live with those faults

without trying to change them?

4. How do I feel when we are apart? Do I miss this person? Do I still love him or her? (Sometimes it can be good to spend time apart from each other to see if absence really does make the heart grow fonder.)

5. How does this person act around his or her parents? Around my parents? Around our friends? Do my parents and friends like this person? These issues can reveal a lot about someone's personality.

6. Is this person the single most important human being in my life? Am I the most important human being in his or her life? Or are they in this just to meet their own needs?

7. Would this person still love me even if there was no physical gratification in it for him or her? Would I still love in return? Of course sex is very important in marriage. We will talk about that in the next chapter. But some people place such an extreme emphasis on the physical that the other aspects of the relationship—the psychological and spiritual—become clouded and distorted. So this is an important question to ask to help put the relationship in proper perspective.

8. Can I honestly envision myself enjoying spending the rest of my life with this person?

Those are some questions that we suggested. If you are interested in knowing more on the topic "Are We Really in Love?" we can recommend an excellent book. It is by a well-known author, Dwight Hervey Small, who teaches marriage and family courses at Westmont College in Santa Barbara, California. His book *Design for Christian Marriage* (Revell) has an excellent chapter on love versus infatuation.

Perhaps the best advice we can give is to wait. Take time to really get to know each other. Love is not an instantaneous flash! It is a *process of growing together in intimacy*. The more time you give it, the better chance you will both have of making the best decision.

What if it doesn't work out? What if you realize that you're not really suited for each other even though you had hoped you were? You should not get married, of course. But you do not necessarily have to assume that you are a failure or that the relationship was a waste. Rather, maybe you can say, "We learned." "We learned about ourselves, about love, and about relationships." Maybe this relationship helped to prepare you for that special person you may eventually marry. Because, you see, preparing for marriage is not just a matter of finding the right person. It is also a matter of *becoming* the right person.

CHAPTER FIVE

WHY SEX?

To begin with, it seems logical to ask a basic question: "Why sex?" In his best-selling book *Everything You Always Wanted to Know About Sex But Were Afraid to Ask,* David Reuben, M.D., discusses three distinct types of sexual intercourse. These three types parallel what we will call three purposes of sex.[1]

Pleasure

One of the main purposes of sex is pleasure. Sex is fun! Unfortunately, not everyone has always agreed. Before World War I, for example, many authorities believed that "sexual feeling in young women in love was pathological and abnormal."[2] Though some today still seem to want to keep the pleasure of sex a secret, folks have known about it for ages! In fact, some of the best sex manuals ever written were produced several thousand years ago. Consider these remarks from one ancient sage:

Drink water from your own cistern,
And fresh water from your own well.
Should your springs be dispersed abroad,
Streams of water in the streets?
Let them be yours alone,
And not for strangers with you.

Let your fountain be blessed,
And rejoice in the wife of your youth.
As a loving hind and a graceful doe,
Let her breasts satisfy you at all times;
Be exhilarated always with her love.[3]

A sociology professor in Illinois told us that during each term she reads excerpts from another ancient Mideastern love song to the students in her marriage-and-family courses. In one part of this love song, the writer lets us eavesdrop on a beautiful and passionate romance. First, the woman revels in her lover's attributes:

My beloved is dazzling and ruddy,
Outstanding among ten thousand.
His hand is like gold, pure gold;
His locks are like clusters of dates,
And black as a raven.
His eyes are like doves,
Beside streams of water,
Bathed in milk,
And reposed in their setting.
His cheeks are like a bed of balsam,
Banks of sweet-scented herbs;
His lips are lilies,
Dripping with liquid myrrh.
His hand are rods of gold
Set with beryl;
His abdomen is carved ivory
Inlaid with sapphires.
His legs are pillars of alabaster
Set on pedestals of pure gold;
. . . His mouth is full of sweetness.
And he is wholly desirable.
This is my beloved and this is my friend.
. . . I am my beloved's and my beloved is mine.[4]

Later he praises her beauty:

How beautiful are your feet in sandals,
O prince's daughter!
The curves of your hips are like jewels,
The work of the hands of an artist.

Your navel is like a round goblet
Which never lacks mixed wine;
Your belly is like a heap of wheat
Fenced about with lilies.
Your two breasts are like two fawns,
Twins of a gazelle.
Your neck is like a tower of ivory,
. . . The flowing locks of your head are like
purple threads;
The king is captivated by your tresses.
How beautiful and how delightful you are,
My love, with all your charms!
Your stature is like a palm tree,
And your breasts are like its clusters.
I said, "I will climb the palm tree,
I will take hold of its fruit stalks."
Oh, may your breasts be like clusters of the vine,
And the fragrance of your breath like apples,
And your mouth like the best wine![5]

To her partner's charms, the woman replies:

I am my beloved's,
And his desire is for me.
Come, my beloved, let us go out into the country,
Let us spend the night in the villages.
Let us rise early and go to the vineyards;
Let us see whether the vine has budded
And its blossoms have opened,
And whether the pomegranates have bloomed.
There I will give you my love.[6]

No doubt about it—sex for those two was dynamic! Dr. Reuben calls this aspect of sex "funsex." Sex is meant to be pleasurable.

Unity

Another purpose for sex is to promote oneness or unity. Nearly 3500 years ago a learned Hebrew leader wrote, "For this cause a man shall leave his father and his mother, and shall cleave to his wife; and they shall become one flesh."[7]

One friend asked, "Why do some people make such a big deal out of intercourse when all it is is mere physical contact?" This Hebrew writer was saying that when a couple unites sexually, it involves a lot more than "mere physical contact." A whole lot more. According to his view, sexual partners, whether or not they are married, become "one flesh" with each other. Each gives a part of himself to the other person. They become united, they become one. Each becomes part of the other.

Another term often used to describe sexual union is the term "to know." When partners enter into sexual intercourse, they enter into one of the most intimate, personal relationships known to humans. Each reveals an intimate part of himself to the other. Each gains an interpersonal knowledge of the other. Sexual intercourse in marriage is designed to promote oneness and unity through this interpersonal knowledge.

Sex therapists William H. Masters and Virginia E. Johnson touch on this concept of unity in their book *Human Sexual Inadequacy.* In their chapter on treatments for female orgasmic dysfunction, they explain that it frequently helps to assure the wife that once intercourse has occurred, she and her husband belong to each other sexually. They add, "When vaginal penetration occurs, both partners have literally given of themselves as physical beings, in order to derive pleasure, each from the other."[8]

"The two shall become one flesh."

Procreation

A third purpose of sex is procreation: propagation of the species. Reproduction, or "reprosex," as Reuben terms it, is how we all got here. In ages past, and still in some cultures today, parents have been concerned with multiplying the population. Most agree, however, that with the world population at over four billion and climbing, our need is not to multiply the race but simply to continue it.

So then sex is for pleasure, unity, and procreation. A question you might be asking at this point is, "How can *I* have a dynamic sex life? How can I get the *most* out of sex?" Chapter 6 gives some proven methods that may surprise you!

CHAPTER SIX

GETTING THE MOST OUT OF SEX

Of all the recent notions about sex that have been given publicity in recent years, none is more harmful than the idea that a poor sexual relationship can be "cured" by learning technique from a book—any book. . . . An emphasis on the importance of technique is characteristic of so much that passes for good advice today. Nothing good going to happen in bed between a husband and wife unless good things have been happening between them before they get into bed. There is no way for a good sexual technique to remedy a poor emotional relationship. For a man and a woman to be delighted with each other in bed, both must want to be in that bed—with each other.

Just opinion or mere conjecture, you say? The above paragraph is directly quoted from *The Pleasure Bond*, a book by Masters and Johnson, the world-famous sex therapists in St. Louis.[1]

One way not to have a dynamic sex life is to concentrate on technique alone. Don't misunderstand us—there is nothing wrong with learning sexual technique, especially the basics. An understanding of sexual physiology can definitely aid a sexual relationship. Indeed, ignorance concerning sexual organs and their functions has produced a great deal of frustration in the past. (This has been especially true when sexual myths have blinded men from helping women achieve sexual climax, or blinded women from feeling that pleasure in sex is good.)

But technique in and of itself is not the answer. A better technique does not guarantee a better sex relationship. So what does? We have found in our marriage (and many professional counselors agree) that the qualities that contribute to a successful sexual relationship are the same ones that contribute to a successful interpersonal relationship.

Mutual Relationships

Dr. Theodore Isaac Rub. , a New York psychoanalyst, writes that "There is nothing more important in human existence than mutual relationships. Our emotional and our physical well-being are deeply affected by how we relate to other people."[2]

Masters and Johnson have found relationships to be vital in the treatment of sexual problems. As the authorized synopsis of their book *Human Sexual Inadequacy,* states:

Sexual interaction requires the involvement of two people. Isolating one partner in therapy often breaks down whatever communication existed between them before. Masters and Johnson have established that it is the relationship which must be treated if sexual function is to be restored. This is why both partners must be present in therapy. They stress that when a relationship has disintegrated totally or when there is profound disinterest from either partner, therapy is useless.[3]

Elsewhere, these famous therapists note the close link between partners' overall interaction and their sexual interaction. They write:

Actually, the marital incompatibility that brings the couple to the physician usually is not primarily of sexual origin. Sexual incompatibility may well be the secondary result of marital disagreement over such problems as money, relatives, or child care.[4]

Joanne and Lew Koch, authors of *The Marriage Savers,* have

done extensive research into the various approaches to marriage counseling used in the United States. They feel that empathy—identifying with the thoughts, needs, and wishes of another person—is crucial to a successful relationship. Writing in *Psychology Today*, they quote sex educator Jessie Potter as saying, "We are looking for a level of intimacy that no other generation has expected out of marriage." Then the Kochs comment, "But informed sex cannot carry the entire burden for the intimate relations today's couples are seeking. Intimacy requires that each partner understands the other's needs and feelings; it demands empathy."

They continue, "At Pennsylvania State University, psychologist Bernard G. Guerney, Jr., is convinced that empathy is the key element in marriage, a quality that is far more valuable when it comes from one's spouse than when it emanates from a paid professional, no matter how skilled."[5]

Your Most Important Sex Organ

Sex, you see, involves nearly every aspect of your being. It's not just a physical phenomenon; it is linked to your total person. In fact, as Josh McDowell in his movie *The Secret of Loving* brings out quite emphatically, "Your most important sex organ is your mind!" Dr. David Reuben also asserts, ". . . the most important sexual organ of all . . . [is] the brain. The mind exerts ultimate control over the pelvis. Ask anyone who has been jolted by the jangling telephone at the critical moment of intercourse. Sometimes when the baby wakes up, the sexual organs go to sleep."[6] He feels that the mind and the quality of the emotional relationship play a major role in sexual problems. Of male impotence, he writes, "About five percent of impotence is on a physical basis."[7] Of female sexual problems, he emphasizes the crucial place of emotions: "Sex without emotional feeling soon becomes sex without physical feeling. Selecting a partner whom she can love and respect is one basic thing a woman can do to minimize orgasmic problems."[8]

Qualities such as love, commitment, and communication will help any relationship develop to the maximum. They are keys to fulfilling sex. Let's consider them.

Love and Sex

Earlier we dealt with the importance of love. Probably you can see how unconditional love will help a sexual relationship. In order for sex to be most fulfilling, it should be experienced in an atmosphere of caring and acceptance. Psychiatrist Alexander Lowen, in his book *Love and Orgasm*, recommends:

Intercourse should not be engaged in under conditions of tension and strain. The relationship between the sexual partners should be one of ease and confidence. Otherwise, the sexual act loses its quality as an expression of love and becomes a compulsive "acting out" of ego drives.[9]

Dr. Reuben wisely adds, "In sexual intercourse, real human emotions can make up for any lapses from perfect form. Even if technique lacks perfection, love and tenderness can fill in the gaps."[10]

Partners are bound to make mistakes—no one is perfect. It is important that each be willing to accept, forgive, and give in an understanding way regardless of the other's shortcomings. When sex is viewed in this context, it becomes not a self-centered performance but a significant expression of mutual love.

Commitment

A second quality besides love that is essential for a strong relationship and fulfilling sex is commitment. We are talking not merely about a commitment to a piece of paper (the marriage license) or an institution (holy matrimony), though we feel that these are important. Rather, we are referring to a deep, abiding commitment to another person as a human being. If two people are completely committed to each other, their relationship will be strengthened. If each knows that the other will support him (her) and show concern and not desert him under pressure, they will be able to function as a team. Trust brings them closer together.

In football, when a quarterback steps up to the line of scrimmage and sees a wall of giant defensive linemen ready to gobble him up, one of the reasons he is willing to take the ball from the center is that he knows there are five offensive linemen who are committed to protecting him. Mutual commitment gives each a feeling that his partner is for him, that he is on his side. Without it, neither will be able to live with maximum confidence that the relationship is secure. The fear may exist, that should they encounter a trial, the other may not be there for support. This uncertainty can erode their bond.

One husband explained the value of commitment (and the trust it involves) in his marriage:

> If I confide something personal to my wife, it helps me to know that she's not going to tell the next-door neighbor. If she goes shopping for a couple of hours, it helps her to know that I'm not going to sell the house and leave town with the bankbook before she gets back!

If partners trust each other, they will be encouraged to share and give of themselves completely. If they don't trust each other, even the smallest suspicions can inhibit their openness and frankness. They may find it hard to live in the same house, not to mention sleeping in the same bed.

Contracts

Some people ask, "What about the idea of a renewable-contract marriage? This plan gives you a chance to sign a limited contract and then decide at the end of two years, five years, or ten years if you want to continue." A big problem we see in this is that such arrangements are founded neither on unconditional love nor on total and permanent commitment. Some may say, "Can't I have unconditional love in my contract marriage?" We say no, because it is not unconditional. It is saying, "I love you . . . until you do something I don't like." It's "I love you *if*." Real unconditional love demands permanence. "But," you ask, "suppose both partners *agree* to separate at the end of five years?" You can't predict what will happen when you enter into the contract. Five years may pass and one partner may want to continue while the other does not. Someone may get ill or injured. No contract can protect against that. While commitment is not a guarantee against pain, it does help to diminish the risk.

Commitment and Sex

Total, permanent commitment is important in sex, too. It brings security to each partner. It frees each from feeling that he must strive or perform sexually to keep the other. Feeling a conscious or subconscious pressure to perform well in bed so as not to lose a partner's affection can cause great fear. One or both can worry that a sexual blunder might end in a severed relationship. Performance fear is one of the greatest causes of sexual failure;[11] a lack of commitment can backfire and produce a lack of sexual satisfaction. Psychiatrist Lowen writes, "In the absence of total commitment to the sexual act and to the person who is one's partner, a satisfactory experience cannot be expected."[12]

Mutual commitment frees people from bondage to performance fears. It releases them to enjoy each other. Masters and Johnson note:

> Total commitment, in which all sense of obligation is linked to mutual feelings of loving concern, sustains a couple sexually over the years. In the beginning, it frees them to explore the hidden dimensions of their sexual natures, playing with sex as pastime and passion, seeking the erotic pleasures that give life much of its meaning. Then, when carrying the inescapable burdens that come with family and maturity, they can turn to each other for the physical comforting and emotional sustenance they need to withstand economic and social pressures that often threaten to drain life of all joy. Finally, in their later years, it is in the enduring satisfactions of their sexual and emotional bond that committed husbands and wives find reason enough to be glad that they still have another day together.[13]

Commitment breeds satisfaction.

Communication

Besides love and commitment a third quality that is essential for a strong relationship and dynamic sex is *communication*. Even if partners share love and commitment, this is not helpful enough unless they communicate it by what they say and do. Simply saying "I love you" can do wonders. By the way, it helps to say it often. One exasperated husband complained, "I can't understand why all the time my wife wants me to tell her I love her. I told her I loved her the day we got married, and until I take it back, it stands the same!" Obviously that fellow had a *lot* to learn about communication!

Showing love by your actions also helps to strengthen a bond. Kind deeds and occasional gifts work like glue. Dividing up the household chores, even if it means sacrifice, gives partners an opportunity to say (through their actions) "I care about you." We try to do that in our home. We share the laundry and housecleaning responsibilities. Linda does the cooking; Rusty does the dishes. We both agree that Linda is the better cook and Rusty is the better dishwasher!

Verbal support and encouragement to pursue an outlet which one finds meaningful can increase excellence and fulfillment. "I'm behind you all the way." "I think you are a fine writer, speaker, counselor, athlete, student, businessperson, etc." Words like these from an understanding mate can provide the impetus needed for success and tend to draw the couple closer together.

Communication and Sex

Sex therapists have found that clear communication is essential to a most fulfilling sex life. For example, Atlanta psychologist Daniel G. Brown, writing about solutions to sexual inadequacy, points out:

A suggestion that has been advocated by a number of workers . . . is that of helping establish or re-establish effective channels of communication with the husband or wife. In a sense, this factor seems so obvious that it hardly deserves mention; yet many couples seen in marriage counseling, even though they may be able to talk about practically anything else that concerns them, are unable to talk to each other about their most intimate relations.[14]

Sexual partners who want maximum fulfillment should seek to develop open, honest, clear communication, especially in the bedroom. Each should tell the other what pleases him (her) and not expect his partner to read his mind. Open, honest verbal interchange about sexual needs and preferences can help turn a warm relationship into a sizzling romance. In response to the question "What can a woman do to initiate sexual intercourse?" David Reuben writes of "almost unlimited" possibilities. Then he recommends, "Even in bed a wife should let her husband know what she wants and how she wants it. It helps a man to perform better if he is sure he is gratifying his partner."[15] It works both ways.

If a problem arises in our relationship, we have found the need to talk it out and forgive rather than give each other the silent treatment and stew in our juices. Gloria Steinem says that "sex is a form of communication."[16] It sure is. You can bet that if partners are harboring resentment or not communicating with each other verbally, it will show in their sex life. Sex will become a source of anxiety, a bore, or perhaps even nonexistent during that time.

CHAPTER SEVEN

THE CART BEFORE THE HORSE?

A student in the middle of the auditorium raised his hand. He had just heard one of our lectures in his human sexuality class at Arizona State University, and now he had a question: "You've been talking a lot about sex within the confines of marriage. What do you have to say about premarital sex?"

In this book, as in his class, we maintain that sex is designed to work best in a happy marriage, and we recommend that couples wait until marriage before having intercourse. He wanted to know why we felt that way. Probably you do too.

Why wait? All we can do is tell you why we waited and let you decide for yourself. We did wait and we're glad we did. One woman in Philadelphia told Rusty, "You're the first guy I ever heard who said he was a virgin when he married and was proud of it." Perhaps "proud" is not the best word; we're not trying to boast or appear arrogant. But we are very *glad.* There are two big reasons why we waited: 1) there are many practical advantages and 2) the arguments we heard for not waiting weren't strong enough. Let's consider both of these categories.

Practical Advantages

There are *practical* reasons for waiting. Premarital sexual intercourse detracts from a strong relationship and dynamic sex. It can erode the qualities we discussed in the last chapter (love, commitment, and communication), or of necessity it can be practiced without them.

Of course there are several different levels of premarital sexual experience, ranging from casual promiscuity to intercourse in a deep, meaningful relationship. Not all of these practical problems apply to all levels of premarital sex, but there are problems with each level. Hopefully this will become apparent as we proceed.

Love. All too often, premarital sex is loveless. It can be exclusively a self-seeking, self-gratifying situation. After intercourse one partner is saying "I love you" and the other is thinking "I love it!" That's not always the case, though. Sometimes genuine love exists. Is it then okay to go all the way? We'll return to that question shortly.

Commitment. Premarital sex often exists in the absence of total and permanent commitment. This can shake the confidence of both partners and make the relationship less than secure. Performance fears can set in. While the couple is unmarried, there can always be the nagging thought, "If he (she) has done it with me, who else has he slept with?" Suppose they marry. Each may think, "If he (she) was willing to sleep with me before we got married, how do I know he won't sleep with someone else now that we are married?" Doubt and suspicion can chip away at their relationship.

Does premarital sex *now* mean extramarital sex *later?* Statistics say that it increases the chances. Kinsey found it to be so.[1] *Redbook* magazine, reporting on a study of 100,000 women done by a professional sociologist, put it like this: "Premarital sex . . . does not necessarily lead to extramarital sex—it simply increases the odds that it will."[2]

Learning to control your sexual impulses before you marry is a good way to help learn to control them after you marry. It not only helps give you the confidence that you can do it, but it also helps show your partner that you *will* do it. Linda states, "When Rusty travels at times without me the thought never enters my mind that he might sleep with someone else. If he lasted past his midtwenties without sexual intercourse, and there was a lot of opportunity then, I have confidence that he will maintain his faithfulness to me now."

Communication. Premarital sex can also inhibit clear communication. This is especially true when there is fear or lack of security in the relationship. He might figure, "Has she slept with anyone else?" She may wonder, "How do I compare with his other women? Does he tell them how I perform in bed?" Each becomes less open, and communication dwindles. Sometimes couples who have difficulty communicating in their relationship turn to sex for help. But poor communication makes for poor sex. Bad feelings result, communication deteriorates, and so does the relationship.

In short, premarital sex puts people at a disadvantage. It lessens their chances to experience maximum unity and pleasure. One young woman expressed it succinctly. After a lecture on sex in her university classroom, she said:

I understand what you're saying about unity or oneness. I've had several different premarital experiences, and I know that each time I've left a part of myself with that person emotionally. What you're saying is that you wanted to save yourself to be able to give yourself completely to your spouse.

That's exactly it. We're not claiming that premarital sex completely eliminates the possibility of a fulfilling sex life in marriage. But it does build factors into the relationship that can be difficult to overcome. "Agape" love is important to have, but we are all fallible humans and subject to mistrust. Often the mistrust or doubt is not a huge, overriding compulsion that totally destroys the relationship, but a tiny thought that flickers through the mind in an instant. Sexual intercourse is so sensitive that sometimes just this tiny thought can kill the sexual stimulation. In other words, anything that will potentially undermine the relationship or hamper the sexual fulfillment can best be done without.

Arguments for Not Waiting

There is a second reason why we waited: none of the arguments other people were giving for premarital sexual intercourse were strong enough. We consider ourselves thinking people. Probably you feel the same about yourself. We like to give other ideas a chance, so we tried to think through various reasons for premarital sex. We found that none of them were convincing. Of course, it's always easy to rationalize in the heat of passion and say it's right. That is why it is important to decide *beforehand*—to think with your brain instead of your glands. Consider just some of the arguments that people use.

The statistical argument:[3] "Everyone else is doing it."

Everyone else is *not* doing it. Some studies have shown high percentages, but we've never seen one that says 100 percent. (More young people wait than you may realize.) Besides, even if "everyone else" were doing it, that is a lousy reason for doing anything. Suppose 90 percent of the people in the United States developed ulcers. Should the American Medical Association rewrite the medical texts to state that it is healthy for people to develop ulcers and recommend the ten best ways to develop ulcers?[4] What if 95 percent of the German people decided that Hitler's extermination of the Jews was a good thing? Would that make it right? Of course not! As Masters and Johnson ask, "Is the frequency with which something happens a reliable indication of its value?"[5]

Some have challenged these comparisons by saying, "You're equating sex with sickness and evil (ulcers and Hitler). The analogies aren't fair!" Our intent is not to equate sex with sickness and evil. We don't use those illustrations to prove that premarital sex is wrong. The point is that "just because everyone else is doing it" does not make it *right*. You need a better reason. Some have called this "everyone-else-is-doing-it" argument the "sociological argument," since many students refer to sociological studies in attempts to justify premarital sex. One sociology professor advised a change in terms. "This is an erroneous title," wrote the professor; "this is a statistical ploy, *not* a sociological argument.

The cultural argument: "Premarital sex was acceptable in many cultures of history and is in many primitive societies today. Moral values depend on the culture."

There is no denying that some ancient societies condoned

premarital sex,[6] and that even today some primitive cultures accept premarital sex. For example, the natives of the Trobriand Island in the South Pacific expect their children to shop around sexually before marriage.[7]

But these cultural arguments are really variations of the statistical argument. They basically say that "if lots of other people do it, it must be okay." The only differences are in time and location. The historical variation says, "People used to do it in the past." The "modern-primitive-tribes" variation says, "People still do it in other places now." But, as with the statistical argument, popularity is not necessarily an indication of value.

Some use these cultural examples to attempt to justify abolition of *all* moral values. But sociologist Arnold Green notes that every society approves of some kinds of sexual activity and disapproves of others.[8] For example, he notes that the Trobriand Islanders have strict sexual regulations. "Incest taboos [sexual relations with close relatives], particularly between brother and sister, are severely enforced. It is considered highly improper for any grown or married person to mingle with the young unmarried. Lovemaking is a private affair and public displays of affection are in extreme bad taste. . . . Strangely enough . . . premarital motherhood is considered reprehensible. Adultery is unmentionable in polite conversation, and is nearly unknown, and public opinion falls harshly upon the offenders."[9]

Modern cultures and subcultures have their standards, too. Green points out, "Even those groups who vagrantly violate the common moral norms must preserve their own specialized moral norms; members of a criminal gang should not 'squeal' on their associates."[10] Few people today place great value on robbery or rape. Thus, the question is not *whether* to draw the line but *where* to draw the line.

Where a culture draws the line can have important consequences. Dr. Evelyn Millis Duvall, internationally respected authority on sex and family life, aptly explains this in her book *Why Wait Till Marriage?*

Dr. J. D. Unwin, The British scholar, studied eighty civilizations ranging over the past four thousand years. He was impressed with the fact that society chooses either sexual promiscuity and decay, or sexual discipline and creative development. He concludes, "Any human society is free to choose either to display great energy or to enjoy sexual freedom; the evidence is that it cannot do both for more than one generation."[11]

The biological argument: "Sex is a biological need like the need for food, air, and water. When I have the impulse, why not satisfy it?"

There are several problems with this. You can't live without food, air, or water. Believe it or not, you can live without sex.[12] Usually eating, breathing, and drinking do not hurt other people; premarital sex can.

If you had the impulse to hit someone else or commit murder, should you do it? Dr. Duvall quotes Dr. Povl W. Toussieng, a Danish psychiatrist at the famous Menninger Clinic in Topeka, Kansas:

The history of mankind is man's struggle against his impulses. He has never completely won that struggle and there are many defeats, but we cease to be human if we merely give in to our impulses. On that basis, speaking only as a psychiatrist, I would say to youngsters about premarital intercourse: "You shouldn't."[13]

Sometimes single people will go so far as to say that if a member of the opposite sex does not give them sexual release, their "health will be dangerously impaired." Robert Bell, Temple University sociologist, quips that there appear to be no records of hospitalizations because sexual outlets were refused![14]

The psychological argument: "Sexual restraint is bad for me; it hurts my psyche. Sexual expression relaxes tension and is psychologically healthy."

Consider how some of the experts respond to this line of reasoning. Sociologist Herbert J. Miles, Ph.D., in his book *Sexual Understanding Before Marriage*, emphatically states: "There is not scientific evidence that premarital self-control is detrimental to normal emotional life or a hazard to successful marriage."[15] Dr. Duvall writes, "Is sexual restraint bad for you? The answer is a simple 'No.' It does not hurt you to inhibit your sexual feelings. Restraining sexual impulses harms neither males or females, old wives' tales notwithstanding . . . . Inhibitions do not necessarily make you nervous . . . . You are in much greater danger of becoming a nervous wreck when you feel guilty about your behavior, as many a psychiatrist can tell you."[16]

Psychiatrist Alexander Lowen notes that some people want to put the cart of sexual fulfillment before the horse of psychological health. He writes, "The full orgasm, as I described it, is an index of emotional health . . . . However, orgasm is the *result* of, not the *means*, to a complete life. It is a mistake to regard orgasm as having some mystical power to resolve personal problems. The emphasis of a rational approach to emotional illness should be upon the conflicts and schisms that rend the unity of the modern personality and not upon orgasm or orgastic potency."[17]

Do you have psychological tension from a strong sex drive? Hearty physical exercise can often help release it. Premarital intercourse can generate a psychological tension that many people cannot cope with.

The contraceptive argument: "With modern contraceptives, there is no longer any fear of pregnancy."

There is always a chance of pregnancy! No contraceptive is 100 percent foolproof. A lot of married couples have had "little surprises." According to two sociologists at Johns Hopkins, "about 65% of all *marital* first pregnancies are unintended."[18] During the week of one of our lectures at Sacramento State University, a young couple discovered to their complete surprise that the wife was pregnant. They had only been married a few months and had intended to postpone parenthood for awhile. They were shocked. After the lecture the husband said, "Now I know how it feels to be a statistic!" At least their child will have the benefit of being raised in a loving family. Not all are that fortunate. Even if a person chooses abortion (and we're not suggesting it), it can still be emotionally painful.

Despite all the modern contraceptives, there are one million teenage pregnancies in the U.S. each year.[19] How many of these pregnancies are due to ineffective use of contraceptives rather than failures of the devices themselves? It is difficult to tell.

Failures can be due to human, mechancial, or chemical factors. Nevertheless, there are failures. Those who feel that modern contraceptives have eliminated all unwanted pregnancies are only fooling themselves. Even to assert that the risk is worth it can be dangerous, for one tiny failure can have serious repercussions.

True, it does take many thousands of male sperm to enable just one sperm to fertilize a female egg. But sometimes that one sperm can get through in ways we would never imagine. Dr. Reuben gives an example in which a young single woman was very upset upon learning she was six weeks pregnant. She and her partner never even had intercourse. They had merely engaged in some heavy (and apparently partially nude) petting, but she pushed him away before he reached a climax. Reuben explains what happened:

> That first treacherous drop claimed another victim. The initial secretion (from the male) originating at the bulbourethral glands appears shortly after erection. No more than an expectant drop at the end of the penis, it can contain as many as 50,000 sperm. If these are wiped against the vulva by an aggressive penis, only one of the kicking, squirming swimmers needs to snake its way up the vagina into the cervix.[20]

Granted, this is a rare case, and the odds against it happening are great. But if a pregnancy can occur *without* intercourse, one must seriously consider the risk *with* intercourse, even when contraceptives are employed.

Incidentally, did you know that, according to one health official, venereal disease (such as gonorrhea and syphilis) is "as prevalent now as the common cold"?[21] An article in *U.S. News and World Report* compared reported cases of the most common major infectious diseases in the U.S. over a recent ten-year period (1966-75). Every disease except the current "leader" showed a marked decrease or at least a leveling off during that period. The leader? Gonorrhea, with almost *one million* cases reported in 1975! In second place was syphilis, with just over 80,000. The closet third was mumps, with 59,647.[22]

But these are only the *reported* cases of VD. One researcher estimates that in 1975 in the U.S. there were over *three million new cases* of VD.[23] Using the three-million figure, that is an average of over five new cases every minute! During the time you are reading this chapter, there will be 100 new cases of VD contracted, 150 if you're a slow reader.

The sex-as-rebellion argument: "I'm fed up with my parents and with society's values. I'm going to have sex no matter what they say."

An ancient proverb says, "He who has a cool spirit is a man of understanding."[24] A wise and understanding person will not allow anger or resentment to overrule sound reasoning. Someone who engages in intercourse merely to spite another person or to isolate himself (herself) from home may have to reckon with serious consequences. One young woman in the Midwest told us her story.

I had a frustrating family life, so one night, when I was thirteen, I got pregnant by a man in his forties. We had just met that night and I figured if I got pregnant it would get me away from home. We married when I was fourteen. Now I'm thirty-one, have a seventeen-year-old son, and a husband in his 60's. Life seems miserable. We are on the verge of a divorce. I wish I had thought carefully and taken time before I made that decision when I was thirteen.

Granted, this is an extreme example. But sleeping with someone out of rebellion seldom produces lasting good.

The hedonistic argument: "But it feels so good!"

Ernest Hemingway said, "What is moral is what you feel good after, and what is immoral is what you feel bad after."[25] Our question is, "How *long* after?" What feels good for a few seconds or minutes may leave you feeling miserable for years.

Besides the possible guilt, one common long-range problem resulting from sleeping around is flashbacks. Each time a person has sexual intercourse with a different partner, he or she can build mental images of that experience. These images can remain in the conscious or subconscious mind and can easily flash back during future intercourse with a new partner. Who wants to be thinking of past sex partners while he (she) is having sex with his mate? Even worse, who wants his mate to be thinking of past partners?

Self-fulfillment is hard to obtain without self-respect. Even the Epicurean philosophers (the pleasure-seekers) saw the need for self-restraint in some things.[26] They found that sometimes it is necessary to forego short-term pleasure for long-term satisfaction. Sex is fun. But sex in the atmosphere of marriage, where there is confidence and security, is a lot more fun. Also, don't forget the other person. Sometimes one partner's pleasure is the other's misery. How would you like being used as nothing more than someone else's pleasure machine?

The authority argument: "Many authorities recommend it."

Choose a course you'd like to follow, and you'll discover plenty of authorities to lead the way. One famous atheist, who was more honest than many, explained his reasons for his particular philosophic stance. Aldous Huxley wrote:

I had motives for not wanting the world to have a meaning; consequently assumed that it had none and was able without any difficulty to find satisfying reasons for this assumption. . . . For myself as, no doubt, for most of my contemporaries, the philosophy of meaninglessness was essentially an instrument of liberation from . . . a certain system of morality because it interfered with our sexual freedom. . . . There was one admirably simple method of confuting these people [supporters of the accepted political, economic and religious systems] and at the same time justifying ourselves in our political and erotic revolt; we could deny that the world had any meaning whatsoever.[27]

Seldom is a respected authority so frank in admitting his own rationalizations!

Every authority has personal biases. Before we choose to agree or disagree with an "authority," it is important to determine the presuppositions and motives behind that person's reasoning. In other words, we should not only ask ourselves who said it and what was said, but also *why.*

The competitional argument: "If you don't put out, you'll be dropped. There are plenty of others who will."

The person who makes such a statement to a prospective partner appears much more concerned about his or her own kicks than about the other person's welfare. There seems to be an emphasis on a relationship, with unconditional love or total personal commitment. Who would want a partner like that? A person who hears such crass threats should *want* to be dropped.

The approbation (approval) argument: "I need to prove to myself and others that I'm a real man or woman."

Probably few people will admit to this common internal reason. It is often disguised in the form of boasting about one's own exploits. When you hear men or women talking a lot about their sexual conquests, you must wonder how much of what they're saying is true and/or why they're talking so much about it. Perhaps it is to hide some of their own insecurities. Furthermore, with today's emphasis on sexual freedom, those who have lacked opportunity or choose not to become involved sexually often find themselves pressured by society to fabricate a story so as not to be an exception.

Does hopping in bed prove or affirm masculinity or femininity? The attributes that other people associate with masculinity and femininity may be different from what you think they would be. A study in 1976 and 1977 of 28,000 men and women by *Psychology Today* revealed some surprising views on masculinity. The researchers found:

> The Hemingway hero is on the way out. Today, the ideal man combines self-confidence, success, and the willingness to fight for his family and beliefs with warmth, gentleness, and the willingness to lose. The macho male who is tough, strong, aggressive, and has many sexual conquests is not admired by either sex.[28]

Nor did either sex admire "many sexual conquests" in a woman. Instead, both sexes appreciated intelligence, love, warmth, gentleness, and the willingness to stand up for her beliefs in woman.[29]

Becoming a well-adjusted person is the key to becoming a well-adjusted male or female. Sexual intercourse is a risky way to find one's identity. If you are well-adjusted and secure, you probably won't feel the need to prove this by sexual exploits.

The "single" argument: "What if you don't plan on ever getting married?"

One student at the University of Wisconsin asked, "Suppose I never marry. If I have sexual intercourse, you couldn't call it premarital sex. I guess you'd have to call it 'pre-death' sex, or something, because I'll never marry!"

With all due respect to that student, you don't really know whether you'll ever marry. People and situations change. You may think *now* that you'll never marry, but a year or a few years from now you may meet someone whom you want to spend the rest of your life with. (That's what happened to Rusty!) Avoiding intercourse *now* can help prepare for a most fulfilling sex life in that future marriage, as we ourselves have seen. Even if you never do marry, you still could be hurting the other person (who may marry) if you have intercourse.

Interestingly enough, if recent studies are accurate, marriage is still the most popular living arrangement. One study of 1191 students from 14 state universities all across the U.S. found that between 96 and 99 percent of the students said they would like to marry in the future. The students were chosen from human relations courses, and the professor who summarized the study notes that such students "tend to be more liberal in their values."[30] One would think that more conservative students would be even more interested in marriage!

Some cite high divorce rates as an evidence that marriage is no longer a desirable option in today's world. However, as Masters and Johnson point out in *The Pleasure Bond*, the proper way to evaluate divorce statistics is by looking at the statistics on remarriage. They use U.S. census figures to emphasize that "the accelerated divorce rate has been accompanied by an accelerated remarriage rate." They continue:

An estimated eighty out of every one hundred divorced persons remarry—and at least sixty of those eighty marriages prove permanent. Thus the very individuals who theoretically have had the experience needed to evaluate monogamy choose to find another partner rather than live alone, and most of them do their best to make that marriage last a lifetime.

This makes no sense at all if marriage is, as some critics insist, a booby trap. Were that true, a divorced person, having savored the freedom of being single again, would hardly be lured back into matrimonial harness, or, at the very least, they would be less tolerant of constraint and more likely to slip the traces by getting a second divorce. But this pattern is the exception rather than the rule.

Contrary to popular belief, therefore, it seems clear that divorced men and women do not ride on a marital merry-go-round. Evidently experience has taught them that some important and rewarding satisfactions, which cannot be obtained otherwise, are possibilities inherent in a stable sexual relationship. Consequently even after one failure, they consider marriage a major goal in life.[31]

The experiential argument: "I need experience so I won't look bad on my wedding night. Besides, practice makes perfect; I want to please my partner all through marriage."

As previously mentioned, love, commitment, and communication—not just technique—are keys to dynamic sex. Why not learn with your own spouse, together, instead of with someone else's wife or sister or husband or brother? There are several good books on sexual techniques that you can read together several weeks or months before the wedding. Some excellent ones are *The Act of Marriage*, by Tim and Beverly LaHaye; *Sexual Happiness in Marriage*, by Herbert J. Miles, Ph.D.; and *Intended for Pleasure*, by Ed Wheat, M.D., and Gaye Wheat.[32] If you fear that your potential spouse might ridicule you if you make a mistake, perhaps you need to concentrate more on developing your relationship before you agree to marry.

Good sexual adjustment takes time, love, and understanding. A study of approximately two thousand women by the American Institute of Family Relations (AIFR) concluded:

Neither delayed marriage nor lack of previous sexual experience is a hindrance to a woman's good sexual adjustment in marriage. . . . Previous sexual experience of a woman is no help to her in making good sexual adjustment in her marriage.[33]

In a personal interview with Dr. Paul Popenoe, founder of the AIFR, we discussed these findings. He commented that not only does premarital sex not help, but it can also do a great deal of harm.[34]

Some people point to other findings that seemingly contradict the above conclusions. Many cite statistics showing that premaritally experienced women are more likely to have orgasms on the wedding night than are virgins. People sometimes conclude from such results that premarital sex helps sexual fulfillment and adjustment in marriage. But such assumptions suffer from several deficiencies. First, the female orgasm is being used as a measure of sexual fulfillment. But not every female orgasm is fulfilling. Certainly many are, but other subjective factors (such as love, emotion, etc.) also affect how fulfilling the orgasm will be. To base conclusions regarding sexual satisfaction only on an orgasmic count is unwise. Second, and perhaps more important, counting *wedding night* orgasms can give a distorted picture. It takes a little while to learn the ropes. As David Reuben notes:

> Adjusting to a delicate and intimate association like sexual intercourse can take a little time. To expect instant orgasm on the honeymoon is courting disappointment. . . . Only occasionally is ecstasy on the agenda for the wedding night, but that really shouldn't bother anyone. Like any other complex operation, sexual intercourse has a breaking-in period. The couple needs to get used to one another's responses, they must learn to coordinate their sexual reflexes, and sometimes they need to discard unrealistic expectations.[35]

You might *expect* a sexually experienced single woman to have already learned how to have an orgasm. Thus she might be more likely to be orgasmic on the honeymoon or during the early weeks of marriage than the virgin, as is often the case. But the virgins soon catch up. Dr. Duvall writes:

> Dr. Kinsey found that women who had responded sexually before marriage made *quicker* sexual adjustments after they married. But this difference between those with and those without premarital sex experience narrows through the early years of marriage.[36]

In the AIFR study cited above, 28 percent of the virgins and 39 percent of the nonvirgins experienced orgasm soon after the wedding. But in less than a year of marriage, the figures were 68 percent for the virgins and 61 percent for the nonvirgins! After "years" of marriage, 86 percent of the original virgins and 85 percent of the original nonvirgins had attained orgasm.[37] Engaging in premarital sex did not help marital sex!

The compatibility argument: "You try on a pair of shoes before you buy them. We need to experiment to see if we're sexually compatible, especially since marriage is such a big step."

The "try-before-you-buy" idea breaks down because the human plumbing system is very flexible and almost always works. Dr. Popenoe writes:

> Sexual maladjustments are in almost every instance psychological in origin. Those that are based on anatomical peculiarities or incompatibilities are almost unknown in everyday life. A competent premarital examination will prevent most of the few that might otherwise occur.[38]

In other words, separate visits to a physician will do the trick.

Some say, "Okay, obviously sexual incompatibility is *more* than physical—it also includes the ability to give and receive love and joy." That's certainly true, but you don't need to hop in the sack together to find out if you can exchange love and joy. You can find that out by spending lots of time together interacting in various situations (in our culture sometimes called "dating steadily" or "engagement"). Again, premarital sex can erode trust and communication. It's wisest to test your compatibility as persons. Dr. Judson T. Landis found that even "happily married couples take a considerable period of time to work out a mutually satisfying sexual adjustment."[39]

After one of our lectures on a California campus, one young man came to the front and said, "I think you're crazy. You shouldn't marry someone unless you've had intercourse with them first to determine if you're sexually compatible."

We appreciated his honesty, but in addition to what we've already said, consider this. If you plan to base the decision to marry a certain person on one or even several attempts at intercourse, you're only creating problems for yourself. You may be setting unrealistic standards. Good sexual adjustment takes time. How many tries will you take? If some are unsuccessful and you quit, how will you be sure that you haven't quit too soon? You may be creating excessive anxiety by basing such a momentous decision on sex—anxiety that will hinder full response. As we mentioned in the last chapter, the burden to perform well is one of the greatest causes of sexual failure.[40] Your "performance check" can be self-defeating. If you decide that you aren't sexually compatible, based on a few tries, you may be saying goodbye to the partner you should have married if you had waited.

The romantic argument: "But if we're in love, sex will deepen our relationship." (Remember that we said earlier in this chapter that we would return to this question.)

On the contrary, it may drive you apart by producing *suspicion* ("Am I the only one?"), *fear* ("We have no commitment—will he or she leave me?), or *anxiety* ("What if it doesn't work out? Will his (her) future partner learn all about me?").

Besides, sex can cloud the issue. Sex is not the key to love. *Love* is the key to sex. Couples who think that sex is the key to love, that "If we're in love it's okay to have sex" or "We'll use sex to determine if we are in love" may be sorely disappointed. They may discover too late that what they thought were feelings of love were really only charged-up sex sensations. It is better to see that you're emotionally compatible, but it does help create a more free and less confusing environment in which to find out.

Some people may say "But you never really know someone until you've lived with him. Wouldn't it be wise to move in together to see if our relationship (both interpersonal and physical) will work out?" True, living together can help people get to know each other well, as most married couples will admit. But, in light of the temptation of premarital sex in almost all such nonmarital arrangements, the disadvantages far outweigh the advantages. As we've stated above, sex can cloud the issue, and performance fears can yield devastating results. (The next chapter will deal with the "living together" question in greater detail.)

The marital argument: "If we're really in love and plan to get married, why all the fuss over the license and date?

Some studies suggest that from one-third to one-half of all engagements are broken.[41] We both went through broken engagements before we married each other. Robert O. Blood, Jr., in his standard work *Marriage,* says that "intimacy produces more broken relationships than strengthened ones."[42]

One professor says, "Yes, but isn't it usually good for bad engagements to be broken?" True, but we should clarify: that's not the point we're dealing with. We're talking about the person who feels he only wants to sleep with his future spouse and no one else. Marriage plans don't always end up in reality. For the person who desires to have sex only with the one he will eventually marry, it is safer to wait. There can still be the problems of breakdowns in trust and communication. Again, sex can cloud the issue. You see, love can wait to give, but lust can't wait to get.

There is nothing magic about the ceremony or the license—certainly having a loving, committed relationship is most important. But public profession strengthens personal commitment, and this is why a public wedding is important. We stood before a pastor and an audience on that great day of wilting (when the pastor says "Wilt thou?" and be wilted!). We found, as many have, that it takes a certain amount of commitment to publicly declare that you love each other and intend to spend the rest of your lives together. Then, once you've done it, you look back and realize, "I did it," and your confidence in the commitment grows. If you wait to have sex until you've said "I do" publicly, it's a better assurance of commitment for each of you. Of course, this doesn't guarantee that one partner won't leave in the future. Nothing does that. But it does help to guard against it.

Consider this illustration. (For simplicity, we'll give the man's perspective. Women, you can easily adapt it to yours.) In order to logically defend premarital sex, a man must be willing to defend the right of another man to have sexual intercourse with his mother before she was married, with his sister before she was married, with his wife before he married her, and with his daughter before she marries.

Why wait till marriage? As we've said in this chapter, we waited for two basic reasons.

1. because there are many practical advantages, and

2. because none of the arguments against waiting were strong enough.

We're glad that we waited. Some people think that sex with the same partner gets boring. Maybe it does if the relationship weakens, but we've found that, as we grow together, it gets better and better and better. We wouldn't want to have sex with anyone else. We're quite happy with each other.

Sometimes, as we reach this point in our lectures, we find people thinking, "You're a little late for me. I've already been involved in premarital sex. What do you have to say to me?" If those are your thoughts, we have several things to say, but we'll hold all but one for a later chapter. For now, though, the arguments we've been giving for waiting also apply to not continuing. Anything that can undermine the relationship should be avoided. As we've seen, premarital sex can do just that. You must focus on the relationship.

There is actually a third important reason we waited: a moral reason. We are both believers in a Supreme Being, and we saw that God clearly says to wait. In the New Testament alone, some form of the word "fornication" is used at least 44 time. Each time the word is used, the content shows that God is displeased with it. For example, it says "flee fornication"[43] and "abstain from fornication."[44] Of course we realize that you might not agree with this viewpoint at all, and we respect your right to differ. You might think, "I knew it. God doesn't want me to have any fun." Frankly, we wondered about that too, until we realized that the reason that God, as a loving parent, gives negative commands is for *our own good*. He wants us to experience something better! In fact, as we'll see a bit later, He offers something that can be the vital dimension in a dynamic sex life.

CHAPTER EIGHT

THE TIE THAT DOESN'T BIND

"Carol and I had been dating for quite awhile," explained Tom. "We felt we were in love, so living together seemed the natural thing to do. It happened gradually. She was spending more and more time at my apartment and began leaving some of her clothes. Then we decided, 'Why pay rent on two places?' "

"That's right," Carol added. "For now we're not sure about marriage. With the high divorce rate, it makes you wonder if it's worth it. Anyway, we figure that living together will help us decide if marriage would ever be for us."

Cohabitation. It used to be material for national scandal. Now it seems commonplace.

More than one million unmarried cohabiting couples were recorded by the U.S. Census Bureau in 1979. Some suspect that this number may be just the tip of the iceberg, since many cases go unreported.[1] Estimates of cohabitation among university students have ranged from 5 percent to 36 percent, depending on the type of campus and the definition of cohabitation used.[2]

Why the increase? Several factors have prompted the rise. Spiraling divorce rates convince some people that conventional marriage is not working. Increasing numbers of women and men are dissatisfied with traditional marriage roles and they are looking for more liberating lifestyles. They desire emotional intimacy, "trial marriage," sexual satisfaction, or simple convenience. Even the government indirectly encourages cohabitation: some couples pay less income tax by living together than by being married.[3]

Is It Working?

Is living together more fulfilling than marriage? Does premarital cohabitation produce better marriages? Numerous cohabiting couples answer yes on both counts. But, interestingly enough, not all researchers agree.

For example, when Dr. Nancy Moore Clatworthy, sociologist at Ohio State University, began her research into cohabitation, more than ten years ago, she viewed living together as a sensible and positive alternative. Cohabiting couples told her how wonderful their relationships were, and she believed them.

But then she began to see young people "so uptight that they could not be happy."[4] After she tested several hundred people from the university community who had lived together, her findings led her to reverse her position. Dr. Clatworthy concluded that "the things people say living together is doing for them, it is not doing. . . . In many cases, the surface answers in favor of living together were not supported by underlying feelings."[5]

What specifically led her to change her stance? Dr. Clatworthy says that "the most common problems were in the areas of adjustment, happiness and respect."[6] She continues: "We asked questions about finances, household matters, recreation, demonstrations of affection and friends. In *every* area, the couples who had lived together before marriage disagreed more often than the couple who had not. Invariably, the couples who had married first indicated a higher degree of unity on these day-to-day matters in their marriages. But the finding that surprised me more concerned sex. Couples who had lived together before marriage disagreed about it more often. You would assume that this would be an area that could be satisfactorily resolved in a living situation. Apparently it isn't."[7]

Researcher Robert N. Whitehurst of the University of Windsor, Ontario, agrees that "there is not one shred of evidence to support such claims [that cohabitation produces better marriages]." He attributes them to "folklore that may have little basis in reality."[8]

I Love You

What are some of the reasons for the discrepancy between what cohabiting couples say and what recent studies actually show?

Studies suggest—and many people assume—that marriage involves a higher degree of interpersonal commitment than does cohabitation.[9] Many noted authorities agree that a commitment that does not involve permanence is not really built on unconditional love. Such a commitment says, "I love you *if* . . ." "I love you *because* . . ." or "I love you *until* . . ." It is not "I love you *period*."

Often this incomplete commitment is expressed subtly in very tangible ways. One Washington, D.C. woman spoke of her and her "apartmate's" hesitancy to invest in major joint purchases. "I wonder about the emotional significance of our never having bought anything of real worth," she said. "I think it is a sign that deep down we were not entirely sure of going on together."[10]

One writer wrestled with the problem of impermanence in an article entitled, "How to Set Your Sweet Lover's Mind (not to mention your own) at Rest That You'll Be With Her Forever When There's the High Statistical Probability You Won't."[11]

Another spoke of a little voice that whispered, "Maybe he doesn't love you *enough* to marry you."[12]

Ironically, the cohabitation boom has produced a multitude of books and counselors who advise couples to make commitments, even in writing. But these commitments usually concern terms of the relationship, including who gets what if and when they split. Sadly, many cohabitors seem more willing to make commitments to possessions and assigned duties than to each other.

This kind of nonpermanent commitment can take its toll in insecurity ("If I'm really myself, will he (she) leave?") and lack of confidence ("I'm not sure if he (she) will *continue* to stand behind me"). An easier escape route can thwart needed change in the maturing process of both individuals.

For example, when arguments come—and they do in any relationships—a binding commitment forces people to face their differences and work them out together. Without that commitment, the door to separation is easily opened.[13] Partners may split in anger and throw away what could have been a great future. One woman agonized over her own "premarital divorce" in these words: "There's just one catch. A question arises that never goes away, although one learns to ignore it after a time. What if you had pinned yourself down, taken the risk, called in the neighbors, raised the house—would it have mattered? Would it have tipped the balance in some way you could not have foreseen, so that instead of being blown apart, you might have come through—changed, of course, but still together . . . ? Married or single, there is no such thing as a free divorce."[14]

Sex

Impermanence can breed insecurities in the sexual area, too.[15] Though many cohabiting couples do feel a need to be sexually faithful to their partners, often that need is not protected by a permanent promise. One or both may feel freer to roam. As one slightly frustrated partner related, "I decided to make myself more available to other men. . . . We *weren't* married, so why pay marital dues when I wasn't getting the security benefits?"[16]

For the one who attempts to convey a blasé attitude toward his (her) partner's promiscuity, many psychologists offer a warning. People need to feel "special," and to ignore or deny that need can lead to depression, frustration, or eventually all-out war. Sex therapists Masters and Johnson further caution that repressed jealousy can harm both the individuals and the relationship.[17]

Some couples use "sexual compatibility" as a test of potential marital compatibility. They may, however, be creating excessive anxiety by basing such a momentous decision even partially on sex—anxiety that can hinder full response. The burden to perform is one of the greatest causes of sexual failure. A "performance check" can be self-defeating. Commitment is essential to developing the best relationship. As psychologist Joyce Brothers notes, ". . . some counselors believe that 'trial marriage' is a contradiction in terms. Without a firm commitment, they insist, two people cannot really know what the marriage experience is."[18]

Differing expectations of commitment is another commonly mentioned difficulty in cohabitation. Often one partner has more permanent hopes for the relationship than the other. This discrepancy can drive the couple apart.[19]

Nancy Moore Clatworthy sums up the case against cohabitation: ". . . people who were living together [used to] tell me how wonderful it was. They still tell me that. People can always justify what they have done. But the test results showed something different from what they were saying. If it is so wonderful, I asked myself, why are all these things wrong with it? Why do you argue more about sex? Why do you argue more about friends and money? You have supposedly had all this time to get to know each other before marriage. Why do you feel the loss of privacy, and why do you feel dominated if it's so wonderful?"[20]

And, we might add, why do most cohabiting couples separate? One study of more than 2500 American males noted that while 18 percent had cohabitated at some time in their lives, only five percent were doing so at the time of the survey.[21] Some research shows that one-third of living-together arrangements last an average of only 4½ months.[22] This instability causes some authorities to conclude that men and women may flounder from partner to partner in search of the ideal relationship. [23] Such couples may be attempting to obtain the benefits of intimacy without laying the proper foundation of love and commitment.[24]

Concerning this love commitment, scholar Eliezer Berkovits emphasizes: "A love that does not have the courage to commit itself 'forever' is lacking in trust, in acceptance, in faith. Love [when] fully personalized desires to be final, ultimate."[25]

What is the proper foundation for love and commitment? Centuries ago, a wise and respected teacher offered an alternative. He and his followers felt that marriage should consist not of restricting roles but of liberating relationships based on mutual love and giving.[26] They felt further that this union is best evoked and sustained through a public, permanent commitment.[27]

This teacher saw humans as having three facets—physical, psychological, and spiritual—with needs in all three dimensions. Some needs—such as those for security, love, and esteem—are not totally met in even the closest of relationships. Cohabitation is being used to try to meet them, but it is not working. No human relationship, not even marriage, can always provide inner satisfaction or the strength to love unconditionally.

This teacher offered a different solution. He claimed to offer true and lasting emotional satisfaction, and the spiritual power to sustain the love commitment which a healthy marriage requires.[28] He said that what we need is not so much an alternative lifestyle as an alternative *life*—an inner transformation. Maybe his alternative—and he himself—merit investigation. More on that later.

CHAPTER NINE

REAL HARMONY

Darkness came early with the winter nights, and this evening was no exception. It was only 5:30 P.M. when Rusty returned from the office, and already blackness had fallen across the sky that covered our mountain home. When he came in the door, Linda told him that their much-loved cat was lost.

She had walked to the grocery store that morning and the cat had followed. A few blocks from home, the cat had encountered an unfriendly dog and had turned back. When Linda returned home, the cat was nowhere to be found.

That evening we decided we should look again. We wanted to begin right away, since coyotes come out at night in the mountains. They have been known to attack pets—our next-door neighbor lost several cats to coyotes. We started out, flashlight in hand, calling "Here kitty, kitty." We looked, called, asked neighbors, looked, and called some more. No cat.

Finally, just as we were heading home, we heard a very faint "meow." We started toward the sound. The meows became louder until we reached a large tree. We looked up, and there she was, 30 feet up, perched precariously on a branch. Apparently the dog had chased her up the tree, and she had been up there for the last eight hours!

We tried to coax her down, to no avail. None of the homes nearby had a ladder tall enough to reach our frightened feline, so we decided to trudge home and bring our own. Rusty carried the extendable ladder while Linda brought a rope, wicker basket, and flashlight.

At the tree we both struggled to get the ladder up—the tree was on an incline and the tree's branches made maneuvering difficult. Then Rusty climbed, basket and rope in hand, while Linda held the ladder. The plan was to convince the frightened feline to get into the basket. But the cat was not cooperating. She peeked around the limb into the basket as Rusty held it underneath the branch . . . then she backed off.

Finally Rusty dropped the basket, grabbed the cat by the scruff of the neck, and started down. Now, in retrospect, we are sure that if we had been in the cat's place we would have been just as frightened as she was—dangling there by the scruff of the neck, 30 feet off the ground. We probably would have screamed just as loudly as she did. And we probably would have clawed and bitten Rusty's scalp with the same intensity as she did! But we also would have purred just as thankfully as she did when she finally reached the safety of our home.

We carried the ladder, rope, and basket home. Then Linda treated the wounds on Rusty's scalp—the cat had clawed a few nice holes in his head, but Linda's rubbing alcohol kept infection from setting in.

You might wonder, "What is a story about a cat doing in a chapter about marriage?" We have included this simple story to illustrate a principle that we feel is vital to a successful marriage. It is so important that we have tried to place it among the foundational principles that guide our own marriage. The principle we are referring to is *teamwork*.

Teammates

We looked for the cat together. We carried the equipment together. Rusty carried the ladder and Linda carried the rope, basket, and light. Linda held the ladder while Rusty climbed up.

It could have been the other way around (in fact Linda wanted to climb up after the cat herself). But the cat was almost beyond Rusty's reach, and he is nearly a foot taller than Linda. Back at home, Linda treated the wounds on Rusty's scalp. Rusty could have done that, but Linda could do a better job since Rusty could not see the top of his head! The entire operation was a team effort.

Facing Life Together

When we were single, we each knew that if we ever got married, we would want our spouse to be a teammate. We each wanted someone with whom we could share our dreams and aspirations as well as our disappointments and discouragements. We wanted a friend who would accept us just the way we were and yet challenge us to reach beyond even our wildest imaginations of our own potential.

We are thankful that as teammates we are able to face life together. As we have mentioned before, we still have a lot to learn. Any marriage is, at best, a union of two imperfect people. In this chapter we would like to present some helpful ideas relating to becoming better teammates.

Why Marriage?

First, though, a brief word on some of the why's of marriage. We have already alluded to several of the reasons for and benefits of marriage. To summarize, marriage fulfills for many people a deep human need for relationship. It allows us to develop a profound openness with one other person and helps satisfy our quest for interpersonal intimacy.

Marriage, we feel, provides an excellent format for giving and receiving unconditional love, for expressing total commitment, and for developing clear communication. Love, commitment, and communication are vital for a successful relationship, as we have stressed throughout this book. In order for unconditional love to succeed it must be just that: unconditional (or as "less-conditional" as possible). Total, permanent commitment to someone else is the best expression of unconditional love. It frees each partner to be open and honest in communication. In our society, we call this type of permanent relationship "marriage." A happy marriage provides an excellent atmosphere for developing an intimate relationship.

Of course, another purpose for marriage is to provide a positive environment for the growth and maturation of children. Should a couple decide to have children, a happy family is a most effective means of rearing them successfully. Loving parents can provide the necessary balance between compassion and discipline, and a good marriage can become the proper model for a child's own adulthood.

Now a look at four principles on becoming better teammates. They are: learn to communicate, be yourself, work together, and develop relationships rather than roles.

Learn to Communicate

Rusty relates an amusing story from his childhood.

When I was in the eighth grade, there was a girl in my class who had to be the most fantastic girl in the world. (At least that's what I thought at the time. I had not met Linda yet!) And I had the world's biggest crush on her.

I was also very shy. I was afraid to tell her how I felt about her. I hardly ever spoke to her except to say "Hi."

Every day after lunch I used to hang around outside the band room, where she had class during that hour. I hoped I would be able to catch a glimpse of her through the open door. And I wanted to give her every possible opportunity to notice me!

One day in English class we had a spelling bee. She was the captain of one of the two teams, and each captain had to choose sides. Do you know who she chose first? Me!

I was so excited! I was sure this must be love! My mind was filled with plans for the future. I even began to think about marriage. But do you know what happened? I never told her how I felt. At the end of that school year she moved away and I never saw her again.

Do you know one of the main reasons why Rusty and that girl never had a relationship? Because they never really communicated. And that is one reason why so many couples today are having problems—they aren't communicating.

One way to almost guarantee an unsuccessful relationship is to never work at communicating. On the other hand, learning to communicate and developing problem-solving skills can often cut marriage problems in half. (Single people who learn to communicate and solve problems in their dating years can get a head start too!) Some of these hints apply to marrieds, some to singles, and some to both.

Learn to listen. Have you ever been around someone who made you feel as if you were the most important person in the world? He or she probably knew how to listen. Do not always focus the conversation on yourself. Learn to listen and really be interested in what the other person is saying. Once we saw a book entitled *The Awesome Power of the Listening Ear.* That title says it all.

Develop the art of conversation. If you are married, you might ask how your spouse's day went, what has been happening on that latest project she has been working on, or what she would like to do for the weekend. Remember, too, that successful conversation is a two-way operation. One-word answers or occasional grunts from behind the newspaper or in front of the TV do not help communciation flourish a great deal. Sometimes it takes conscious effort for both partners to engage in meaningful conversation. But the effort is worth it if it keeps your marriage from becoming mired in mediocrity.

Too often the only times which married couples allow for communciation are over breakfast, when they are not yet awake, or over dinner, when they are exhausted from the day's activities. Perhaps you need to plan a quiet evening out, a special date, or a secluded weekend at a motel.

Often we are hesitant to say how we really feel about things. Sometimes we fear rejection. At other times our problem is pride—we do not want others to think less of us. Some people are not in touch with their own feelings; this can hamper communication as well. Attempting to live up to someone else's standard of how you should feel and be can also inhibit genuine expression. This is why permanent commitment is so important in marriage. It helps to free each partner so he is able to expose his innermost feelings to the other partner.

Attempt to Understand. When one moves beyond casual dating relationships to more serious involvement or marriage, communication becomes even more complex. Learn to solve problems before they begin. Make sure you really understand the other person's point of view. Here is a helpful problem-solving technique that you can use when you sense conflict developing.

Let's say Rusty and I are having a conversation and we sense tension. Or we have a disagreement and it is about to boil over. We can stop.

I can clearly and simply tell Rusty my point of view. Then he can tell me what he heard me say. Next I tell him if he heard me correctly. Then we reverse the situation. Rusty tells me his viewpoint. I tell him what I heard him say, and he tells me if I understood him correctly.

Try it sometime. You will be amazed how often the disagreement is really just a simple misunderstanding. Of course, if you try this technique and still disagree you have to keep working at a solution.

Good communication is an art, not a sport. It is something you both work at to draw you closer together; it is not a game in which one wins and the other loses. Did you know that often the most difficult thing to give is "in"? Yet "giving in" may be the solution that prevents a minor dispute from totally demolishing the relationship. Learn to say "I'm wrong" and "I'm sorry." It may hurt, but you will be amazed how it can heal. And remember that a good relationship takes two good forgivers. Learn to communicate.

Be Yourself

Another tip for becoming better teammates is "Be yourself." Rusty has some comments on this one.

One of the things I like best about Linda is that she is her own person. She does not fit into anyone else's mold.

During our engagement she was on a university campus in Colorado for several weeks while I had to be away in South Carolina. She made a huge sign for her dormitory window that said LINDA LOVES RUSTY in giant letters that were about a foot tall. It was the talk of the campus!

It has been Linda's personal creativity, her uniqueness, that has made her so successful at so many things. She has had three books published. She has written for major magazines like *Ladies' Home Journal.* She has spoken on university campuses across the country and has appeared on national television. She has done extensive counseling and is an accomplished singer.

My wife is her own person. We don't have to play silly little "pretend" games. We can love each other for who and what we are. If you practice being yourself, you will probably enjoy life a lot more. If you are dating, chances are that your date will like you better too. If you are preparing for marriage, you will want your date to evaluate the *real* you instead of the false you. If you are nearly married or already married, you already know that false fronts become harder to keep up the closer you get. Learn to be yourself in a relationship.

One person related a situation from her life that suggests an important qualification on this theme. She said she used to have trouble with people liking her. That is, no one seemed to! Then she heard people say "Just be yourself, and people will like you." "So," she said, "I tried to be myself. But people still didn't like me!" The point is that some people seem to have an excess of, shall we say, socially undesirable personality traits. For such people the best advice may not be "be yourself" but "work on your own maturity." Certainly this advice could apply to all of us to one degree or another.

Work Together

Another tip for becoming better teammates is to *work together.* If your team is going to be successful, both members need to cooperate. You could both be involved in the same vocation or cause and thus have many daily opportunities for mutual interaction and cooperation. Or, if this is not the case, your home life (or a special project that you work on together) can provide the main stage teamwork. In either situation, *cooperation* is the key.

We are thankful that our situation allows us to work together on different projects. This gives us plenty of practice at exercising give-and-take. For example, we prepare speeches together. Rusty gives an example.

One day I was speaking to a group of university students on a controversial subject. Though many of the students were polite and respected me for holding my point of view, it was obvious that most of them did not agree with me. Their response in the question-and-answer sessions showed that they had not found my lecture to be very convincing.

When we returned home, Linda sat me down and challenged my socks off! She said, "Rusty, you are a good speaker but you are not a great speaker. You could be a great speaker if you worked at it." After my blood stopped boiling, I asked her what she meant. She said, "The reason those students did not find your speech convincing is that you did not work hard enough. You need to thoroughly research that subject and carefully plan your presentation to communicate your views in the most logical fashion."

I had thought myself to be a good "off-the-cuff" speaker. But I gave the matter a good deal of thought. Eventually I decided that she was right. Over the next few months I spent hundreds of hours in researching, sifting information, developing illustrations, organizing my talk, practicing, and polishing. At each step Linda would help. With her usual candor she would say, "This part is great but that part stinks." Back to the drawing board! Finally I had a speech of which we could both be confident.

The difference has been like night and day. Where once audiences were only half with me some of the time, now they seem much more attentive and receptive. I do not claim to be a great speaker yet, but the improvement has been marked. The increased number of invitations, larger crowds, offers to write books, and bookings to appear on television—all of these can be traced, in part, to my willingness to listen to Linda and to work harder on my communicating. I only became willing when my wife challenged me with the need. I'm glad I listen to her!

Linda gives another example from her perspective.

Most of the time when I am working on writing, speaking, or singing, I try to bounce ideas off Rusty. It helps to have someone else as a sounding board, and the fact that we are both committed to the same objectives makes his opinions that much more helpful. I am usually pretty effective at communicating my ideas on paper, but often my work needs a bit of editing. Rusty is fairly adept at editing, and he often helps me in that area. I usually ask him to read my articles and books before I turn them in to the publishers. One time he even stayed up until 3 A.M., on his own initiative, editing one of my books. That not only helped me get the book in on time, but it also showed me how committed he is to my success.

Stop and Smell the Roses

Our work has provided many opportunities for teamwork. The cooperation has also enhanced our marriage. One lesson we've both had to learn, though, is that sometimes outside involvement can get in the way of a marriage. We are both high achievers and very goal-oriented. Sometimes we can become so involved in a particular project that we tend to neglect the other person.

After we had been married for two or three years, this problem became particularly evident. Rusty was heavily involved in several projects at the office and often ended up staying late at work. The pressure he felt plus the tight schedule put a strain on our family life. We found ourselves becoming irritable and arguing more often. Finally Rusty concluded that he should cut back at work and spend more time at home. He realized that any project will always have more areas that can be improved and that he could conceivably spend 24 hours a day at the office and still not get everything "done." Besides, he discovered that the pressure made his work less enjoyable to him than it had been before. And he was reminded by this situation of the need to place his spouse in higher priority than his work. Usually now if friction develops in our marriage, it can be traced to overscheduling.

We have found the need to learn to enjoy things that interest the other person but that may not interest us. Linda likes, among other things, flowers, Christmas trees, nights out, picnics, tender words, and reading books aloud together. Rusty is not especially turned on by most of these. He likes tender words but does not see much point in reading books aloud together. He does like to read books and magazines by himself, though, and one of his favorite pastimes is watching the Miami Dolphins play football. Once he even carried his small portable TV to the airport and arrived three hours before his plane left so he would not miss the game en route to the airport!

We have both had to learn to adapt and to take interest in things that interest the other person. We go on picnics, watch football games together, and sometimes even read books aloud together. (Rusty recently confessed, though, that with one rather lengthy book we had read aloud several years ago, he had read only the first sentence of each paragraph. Linda *had* thought that the author had something unusual about her style, but she had not been able to quite put her finger on what it was!)

One of the best investments we ever made was the purchase of two small mopeds. When the weather permits we love to ride around in the mountains or go down to the beach with the wind whipping past our faces. If we need a break from the pressures of work or life, the mopeds give us an inexpensive way to have fun together. Couples with children especially need these occasional outings in order to rebuild unity and keep romance alive. Remember, a strong husband-and-wife tream usually means a strong family unit.

Whether at work or at play, *cooperation* is essential to building a successful team.

Relationship Versus Roles

Another tip for becoming better teammates is to view your marriage as a relationship rather than a set of roles. By roles, we refer to preset patterns of operating, patterns that sometimes overlook individual differences and needs. In some families, for example, the typical role approach to marriage would view the husband as the leader and the wife as the follower; the husband as the breadwinner and the wife as the homemaker; the husband as the aggressive achiever and the wife as the behind-the-scenes encourager. At the other extreme, some set up roles in which both feel that the wife *must* have an outside job or that spouses *must* share household chores.

We certainly respect anyone else's right to run their marriage as they see fit. Certain couples may be comfortable with the role approach to marriage, and we do not want to criticize them. Our concern, though, is that we have encountered an increasing number of married persons who find the role approach stifling. Sometimes both husbands and wives feel that an over-emphasis on roles causes them to lose an emphasis on their own individuality.

People are unique creatures. Each person has his (her) own needs and talents. Couples should strive to fit together, to find what works best for *both of them*, and not just what works best for one. This is why we prefer to view marriage guidelines in terms of principles of relationship rather than preset role models.

The principles of relationship we refer to are the same ones we have been discussing all along in this book—principles such such as unconditional love, total commitment, and clear communication. A first-century writer expressed it best when he said, "Submit to one another. . . ."[1] Another bit of advice from a similar perspective reads, "Let us consider how to stimulate one another to love and good deeds."[2] Mutual submission and positive encouragement are what we are talking about—not excessive need denial but a willingness to look out for the other person.

Decision Making

We prefer to look at our relationship as a two-way street. In decision making, we try to consider a wide variety of factors—backgrounds, needs, priorities. Rather than ask the question, "How should I respond according to my role as a husband or wife?" We would rather ask, "What would love do?" "How important is this to *both* of us?" "Who is most capable of making the best decision in this situation?" One leader whom we respect said that, in their marriage, if both of them do not feel at peace about a particular course of action, they do not do it. They look for a compromise until both are reasonably comfortable with the decision. Another good practice is to use "trade-offs" for major decisions. This is both fair and mutually supportive of each person's individuality.

Centuries ago a wise king wrote about the importance of teamwork. He said, "Two are better than one because they have a good return for their labor." "For if either of them falls, the one will lift up his companion. But woe to the one who falls when there is not another to lift him up."[3] Two are better than one in decision-making, too. Elsewhere the king wrote, "Without consultation, plans are frustrated, but with many counselors they succeed."[4]

The more advice you can both get, the more effective you will be. A spouse frequently provides a needed check in the decision-making process. Ruth Graham, wife of Billy Graham (and a successful speaker and writer in her own right) says of marital decision making, "If both of you agree on everything, one of you isn't needed!"

Our own decision-making in our marriage has shown us the wisdom of mutuality. For example, one autumn Linda felt that we should buy a house. We had been renting and had thought about buying but had never made the move. Now Linda had found the "perfect" home, but Rusty wasn't interested. He liked the house she had found, but didn't want the hassle of buying and moving. Linda was persistent, though, stressing the financial benefits, the improved location, privacy, timing, etc.

Finally Rusty saw the wisdom of her point of view, and we made the move. It came at a time when were able to get an excellent mortgage rate and a houseful of furniture donated to us by a relative. Since our salary is somewhat modest, those benefits were significant. And today Rusty is very glad we moved. Our current house is much more quiet and private than the previous one—important assets in our line of work, which often requires long periods of study and thinking.

As no section of this book should be considered in isolation, so successful decision-making only works in an atmosphere of unconditional love, total commitment, and good communication.

Good Advice

If you try to reach agreements but find that you reach a stalemate, you may need to seek counsel from someone else.

You can go together to a friend or counselor who perhaps can provide the objectivity you both need. Sometimes in our culture there is a stigma against seeing a counselor about your marriage. Some people feel that one or both partners must have something terribly wrong with them if they go to a marriage counselor. We disagree.

In everyday human interaction, almost anyone can benefit from good advice about dealing with people. Husbands and wives are people too, and an outsider can often help spouses learn more about their mates. Whether the outsider is a trusted friend or a paid professional, the time will often be valuable. We have had several occasions to seek wisdom about our relationship—either for suggestions in solving problems or for guidelines in making the good times better. We don't always agree with the advice that is given, but at other times we find it most beneficial. Don't be afraid to ask for advice. It's *smart* to do so.

CHAPTER TEN

TRUE AND HAPPY

When I married Linda (says Rusty) she promised I would never be bored.

Once in our second year of marriage, I left on a two-week lecture tour while Linda stayed home to tend to some other responsibilities. I left California on a Saturday, flew to Iowa, and checked into a motel in Cedar Falls, a small rural community in the northern part of the state. I was scheduled to speak several times that week at the University of Northern Iowa. That evening I phoned Linda to tell her I had arrived safely.

The next day, after tending to some personal responsibilities, I began my series of speaking engagements. On Sunday evening I returned to the motel around 9:30 P.M. As I inserted the key into the lock, I thought I heard something or someone inside the room. The more I listened, the more it sounded like water running. Had I left the water on in the bathroom?

I turned the key and opened the door. The bathroom light was on and the door was slightly ajar. I could tell that someone was inside. Did I have the wrong room? Was this an intruder? I looked closer.

There was a naked woman in my bathroom!

It was Linda!

She had flown several thousand miles to join me on the lecture tour. She had taken a taxi from the airport and wanted to surprise me. She had hoped to be cleaned up and pretending to be asleep when I arrived. Her plan was for me to find her lying in bed with only her long blonde hair visible to me. I had returned to the motel earlier than she had expected and had partially spoiled the fun. I still was *very* surprised, though!

Yes, Linda promised me I would never be bored having her as a wife. Since that time there has been lots of love, plenty of joy, and loads of surprises. There have even been times I've been discouraged. I've been angry. I've been confused, concerned, even depressed. But I'll have to admit, I have never yet been bored!

Unfortunately, some people do become bored with their mates and seek other partners. The results can often be disastrous. Linda's surprise visit as "the naked woman in the bathroom" has probably prompted most husbands and wives who are reading this now to ask themselves a question: "What would I have done if I had walked in on someone of the opposite sex who was *not* my spouse?" Or, perhaps even more intriguing, "What would my husband or wife have done if he or she had walked in on someone like that?"

Open Marriage

"What do you two think about extramarital sex?" asked the young husband as we talked in our living room. "More and more people seem to be thinking it is okay these days. Some couples even agree, between themselves, that each partner can sleep with other people. And if extramarital sex is acceptable, it seems fruitless to argue about premarital sex or living together."

Our friend's question reflected an increasing national awareness of marital infidelity. A casual glance over nearly any bookrack or magazine stand will do the same. Articles with titles such as "The Pleasures of Sexual Freedom," "Married Men: The Exciting Summer Fling," and "Suburban Mate-Swapping: That Swinging Couple Down the Block" keep the issue in the forefront. Romantic triangles have long fueled the fires of passion for novels, plays, and motion pictures. Previously, the spouse who wandered was often looked down upon for his or her indiscretion, but nowadays the wanderer is often considered the hero. There seems to be an emphasis today on books that encourage infidelity, that even promote it as a solution to marital problems or an aid to personal development.

Just how widespread is extramarital sex? Why are people sexually unfaithful? And can it really do you or your marriage any good?

How Widespread?

Accurate statistics on extramarital sex are hard to come by. Authorities point to difficulties inherent in the method of counting. A major problem is that you have to ask the people themselves. Some individuals may be hesitant to admit an adulterous episode while others may boast about a fling that never happened. Even once statistics have been gathered, there is still the problem of interpreting them. For example, a spouse who was unfaithful only once—and who regrets it—may get lumped together in the count with those who practice infidelity as a way of life. And one's values can change with time. Someone who was previously a "chronic offender" may have changed his or her habits; but this person might be tabulated in a survey merely as having had many extramarital liaisons. Conversely, one who stands for faithfulness today may alter that stance in the future.

Marcia Lasswell and Norman Lobsenz are coauthors of the book *No-Fault Marriage*. She is associate director of the Graduate Program in Marriage and Family Counseling at the University of Southern California. He is a professional writer specializing in marriage and family issues. Together they write that "the most widely accepted figures [on infidelity in the U.S.] . . . indicate that more than half of all husbands and about one-third of all wives have been unfaithful at least once. And those percentages are on the increase, particularly among working wives and couples under 30."[1]

Some other estimates go as high as 60 percent for husbands[2] and 54 percent for wives.[3] Regarding these higher figures, however, Lasswell and Lobsenz are quick to point out an important fact: "What often goes unnoticed . . . is another set of equally reputable studies that report that an overwhelming majority of men and women disapprove of infidelity. One survey shows that 86 percent of those questioned believe extramarital sex is always or almost always wrong. Another 11 percent feel that special circumstances must be considered; they say it is wrong 'sometimes.' Fewer than 3 percent say infidelity is not wrong at all."[4] These writers discuss the difficulties of statistical interpretation (mentioned above) and make a somewhat intriguing assertion: "To many of us who work in this field, all the evidence points to a resurgence of fidelity."[5]

Why People Are Unfaithful

We will leave the statistics debates to statisticians and move to a more personal question: why do married men and women fool around in the first place?

A common motive seems to be to meet a need for self-esteem. One husband, Bill, felt extremely depressed and drained over conflicts at work. "Everything was going wrong at the plant. Suppliers were late, deliveries were fouled up, customers were screaming and threatening to take their orders somewhere else—and it was all on my shoulders. I didn't want to bother . . . [my wife] with what I was going through. That was my first mistake."[6]

Bill went on to explain that the crisis at work brought an emotional crisis within himself. He began to feel drained and found it difficult to handle job-related problems, even though he had once enjoyed solving them. This led to depression and fear. "I would lie awake nights wondering if I could function anymore," he related. "And sometimes I thought, what difference does it make? I used to think I would do something with my life, and there I was worrying about *plumbing* supplies. And I realized that's all I would be doing for the rest of my life."[7]

The only sympathetic ear that Bill seemed to find was his new secretary. They often stayed late to work together at the office. Once she accompanied him to an out-of-town meeting. "Well, that's how it started," said Bill. "Sort of by accident. I mean, it wasn't deliberate or anything on my part. I didn't want *her*. I wanted . . . a release. And I guess I wanted reassurance that I was still worth something, still a man."[8]

Self-esteem needs show up in many ways. For some, as in Bill's case, pressures at work make people question their worth. Others face the often-discussed "midlife crisis"—wondering in their forties if they have really accomplished anything significant or if they still seem appealing to the opposite sex. Sometimes a soured relationship has taken the sizzle out of the marriage bed, and men and women look for a reaffirmation of their masculinity or femininity.

"I Couldn't Break It Off"

One woman in her fifties explained how an affair at first brought a new zing to her sex life. "My husband and I had a good sexual relationship in the early years of our marriage. Then in the eighth year, just after our youngest son was born, I began an affair with my pediatrician. He was unhappily married but had no intention of getting a divorce. That was all right because neither did I. At first it was ecstatic. I discovered a kind of sexual intimacy I had never known. It continued in secrecy for nearly ten years, but as time went on I became more and more afraid of being caught. I felt guilty and I had trouble sleeping. I would get depressed and think it might be better to die. But I couldn't break it off. I didn't want to."

"Finally I told my husband. I felt I had to be honest. He was deeply hurt. 'I can forgive you,' he said, 'but only if this never happens again.'

"That was ten years ago. The distance between us since has been unbearable. We are polite. We go on vacations together. We talk about the children. We even make plans for his retirement. But he never touches me with real affection."[9]

Additional motives for infidelity abound. Some people cite boredom with their mate. Some seek excitement as a change from the monotony of life. Some are lonely and want someone to talk with. Some are merely curious or eager for variety. Some are angry with their mate for being unfaithful and seek revenge through their own infidelity. Some are greedy or are tintillated by the desire to do something forbidden. Some simply yield to the temptation.

And temptations often seem hard to resist, especially in the light of current pressures. Philadelphia psychiatrist Melvin Heller speaks of pressures on the modern man. "The erotic fantasies beaten into him by radio, TV and newspapers create pressures that are impossible for many a middle-aged male to withstand. He's pushed to purchase a brand-new sex life and wife just as he's pushed to buy a new car."[10] Certainly those same pressures affect the modern females as well. Additionally, the popular "soft porn" magazines, amply provided at almost any local supermarket, present idealized sex. In most cases habitual reading of such material keeps the marriage bed frustrating. The wife is not able to meet the unreal standards.

One central question continues to surface among those who have seriously thought through the fidelity issue: "Can one person ever meet all my needs?" Moria, who married at 31 says, "I regard my husband as the most exciting man I have ever known. . . . But is it fair or reasonable to expect one man, no matter who he is, to meet all your sexual needs for a lifetime? Sometimes I worry that the time may come when my husband would not be able to meet my needs. If that happens, I don't know what I'll do."[11]

Do we need more than one sexual partner apiece? Will infidelity help our marriages and enhance our personal growth? Or will the cure be worse than the disease?

Does It Help or Hurt?

A student in Iowa told us, "I cannot believe that a marriage so possessive that the members want to be sure the other partner is having sex only with him or her is in any way maximum." In contrast, Masters and Johnson devote a whole chapter in *The Pleasure Bond* to explaining "What Sexual Fidelity Means in a Marriage."[12] These researchers note many of the problems inherent in extramarital sex. They especially warn against blindly following the advice of modern authors who extravagantly promote it.

Masters and Johnson write of the "human need for the security of reasonable limits in sexual relationships."[13] They stress the importance of "loyalty and faithfulness, honor and trust." "All human association depends on these and other such values," they assert, "and they cannot be ignored in relation to marriage."[14] They note that extramarital sex can be "destructive to the emotional fabric of a marriage."[15] They question the wisdom of those with marital problems who "make the issue seem to be the rightness of extramarital sex—when the issue is really the inadequacy of the marriage."[16] They prefer to emphasize "what makes it [extramarital sex] unnecessary" and to help couples see "how and why the sense of being mutually committed may contribute to the sexual responsiveness of both partners and to the durability of their exclusive relationship."[17]

In their chapters on "Swinging Sex," they relate group interviews with sexual "swingers." Then they comment on the idea, giving some guidelines:

> If in truth swinging is enjoyable for both members of a committed unit, one can only say: how fortunate! But there are a number of important if's—if the extramarital activity (whether it occurs with both partners in the same social situation or with each functioning individually in outside affairs) actually is stimulating to both of them in such a way that it reinforces their desire for each other; if it is an activity that each unequivocally supports for the other, with no doubts and no reservations; and if the extramarital sexual pattern proves over a period of time to strengthen the relationship between the husband and wife, then and only then would this kind of behavior be understandable. These are very special conditions and they are not likely to be met by many couples who engage in this experimental kind of lifestyle.[18]

They also point out the destructive nature of the jealously which, despite frequent denials and rationalizations by the swingers, often pervades such arrangements.[19]

It is noteworthy that, a year after the original interviews with the swingers, Masters and Johnson conducted a follow-up session with eight of the eleven participants (the other three could not be reached). They report:

Without exception, they all indicated that the pace of their sexual activity had slowed considerably; several of them had stopped swinging altogether; and two of the men indicated they were having potency problems.[20]

The researchers noted that their interviews with the swingers do not purport to constitute a representative sample. Nevertheless, they point out that "all but two of the participants . . . emerged from their experiences seeking an improved sense of personal security." Those two, a married couple, said they had stopped swinging because it took too much time. "There are too many other things we want to do," remarked the wife, "and we need time to be alone together."[21]

About Face

Masters and Johnson are not the only authorities who emphasize the importance of sexual fidelity. Ironically, one of the most famous was once best known for advocating *infidelity*. Nena O'Neill coauthored the best-selling book *Open Marriage* in the early 1970s. She stressed the need for freedom from stifling and rigid roles and the need for couples to relate to each other and to selected outsiders and close friends. Additionally, she wrote that getting to know others sexually could be beneficial and rewarding.

Human Behavior magazine reported in October 1978 that Nena had changed her opinion and had concluded that *fidelity* makes for more stable marriages. "O'Neill, who has now written another couples-oriented book, *The Marriage Premise,* found in her research on 250 couples that those marriages ending within two years tended to be the ones that deliberately included some extramarital sex."[22]

In *The Marriage Premise,* O'Neill elaborates, "I have found . . . that as we grow accustomed to the new freedoms and opportunities and how to deal with them, as we become more open to our attitudes about sex, more couples are reaffirming their need for sexual exclusivity."[3] She gives the example of one wife, Connie:

"I didn't think fidelity was important," Connie says, "or that both of us would put it way, way up on our list. When we first got married, I know Paul thought it was important, but I always thought that the double standard was sort of acceptable. I really believed that if Paul was seeing some nurse at the hospital, it wouldn't really bother me. Well, now when I think about it, I know that it would drive me crazy. It would mean that Paul was not Paul, among other things, and I like Paul. As I know him now, he isn't capable of that, and if he did it, too many things would be different."[24]

O'Neill continues, "The assurance of sexual fidelity is still an important and necessary part of most marriages and infidelity an extremely threatening situation . . . . Sexual fidelity is not just a vow in marriage or a moral or religious belief, but a need associated with our deepest emotions and our quest for emotional security."[25]

Feeling Special

Nearly everyone has a need to feel special, to be the most important person in someone else's eyes. Renowned sex therapist Dr. Helen Singer Kaplan writes that "most women find sex with one person they care about the most emotionally satisfying. . . . My view is that most women, and probably most men, strive for a complete relationship with one person."[26] Dr. Hilde Burton, a practicing psychologist and lecturer at the University of California at Berkeley, voices a similar view: "Deep down, most people want to be cherished, and to have a safe setting in which to care for someone."[27]

As we have seen, love, commitment, and communication help produce the strongest, closest bonds and also the maximum sexual fulfillment. The concepts of marriage and fidelity, when properly understood, incorporate the elements that will strengthen and enhance a relationship. Sexual infidelity tends to undermine those elements. It can say to one's spouse, "You are not the only object of my romantic love. You are no longer special to me in that area." It betrays a lack of commitment.

Nena O'Neill was profoundly influenced by her own parents' fiftieth wedding anniversary. As she observed and reflected on their love over the years, she came to appreciate the value of their commitment. "My parents give me warm assurance that two people can care for each other forever. . . . I understand now the full meaning of commitment, of the time together that marriage implies, of being the most important person to someone and having someone as your most important person, of the context of family in which it all takes place. Neither of my parents has lost individuality through their marriage, traditional though it is. If anything, it has reinforced their distinctions to me as individuals."[28]

Infidelity can also hamper communication. The sense of abandonment breeds insecurity and jealousy. "Even when sexual nonexclusivity is agreed upon between partners," says O'Neill, "the same feelings often occur. Resentment, a feeling of rejection, anger and insecurity follows, sometimes as strongly as they do when a clandestine affair is discovered or revealed."[29]

Frederic F. Flach, M.D., in his article "The Case for Fidelity," relates the account of one betrayed husband who said, "I never was involved with anyone other than my wife. When she told me what had been going on, I wasn't surprised. I had a pretty good idea already. I thought of breaking up our marriage, but for a lot of reasons I decided not to. I forgave her, but I could never trust her again nor want to be intimate with her. We do have sex, but it is perfunctory, a matter of marital obligation."[30] Infidelity, in his case, has led to an emotional isolation that inhibited close communication.

What to Do?

What should a couple do if one partner is unfaithful? Certainly the episode can leave deep scars and lasting complications. A detailed list of suggestions would be beyond the scope of this book. However, we would be remiss if we did not make a few comments.

If you are the one who has been unfaithful, the first thing to do is to stop the affair. Then carefully consider if you should take the initiative to clear the air with those you have wronged. Whether or not you should tell your spouse is a complex issue. For example, if the affair took place many years ago and you feel quite certain that your spouse never knew about it, to bring it up now could add an immense burden to the marriage. If you suspect that your spouse does know, it is probably best to admit it and ask for forgiveness. But even if you think that your spouse does not know, there may be cases where it is best to confess. Because each case is so complex, we recommend that you seek the advice of a qualified counselor, minister, or close friend.

If you are the one whose spouse was unfaithful, you should take the initiative to forgive your spouse. You may need to be the one to confront him or her with the problem. It may be painful, but in many cases it can be better than living with duplicity.

A famous novel and motion picture popularized the statement "Love means never having to say you're sorry." We would alter that advice to read like this: "Love means you're glad to say you're sorry when you've wronged your lover but they'll forgive you even if you don't." A good marriage takes two good forgivers!

But forgiveness is only the beginning. How do you repair the broken ties? How do you soothe the hurt? It is rarely easy. Spending time together and working at communication may help. Seeing a counselor may help too. But sometimes there seems to be a need for some kind of change on the inside that allows your memories to heal so you can forget as well as forgive. How can that transformation take place? We will get to that in the next chapter. But before we do, let's return to an important issue.

Is One Partner All I Need?

Earlier we mentioned the common question, "Can one sexual partner ever meet all my needs for a lifetime?" Some have decided "no" and have used that decision as a justification for extramarital sex. They speak of a need for variety in sexual partners in order to achieve sexual satisfaction.

We maintain that the deepest, most fulfilling satisfaction comes from a deeper, closer relationship with one partner. The better two people get to know and love each other, the closer they become and the more freedom they experience in opening themselves up to each other. This freedom is essential for total release in the sexual act.

We believe the one who seeks greater sexual fulfillment through many partners is on a search that will never bring maximum satisfaction. Certainly a new liaison may bring an initial tingle that was lacking in a dull marriage. But soon the mystery wears off and another partner is sought. The process is repeated, but each time the person reaches only a relatively minor degree of closeness with the new partner. His or her promiscuity may reflect not a sexual *maturity* but a type of emotional *immaturity* or isolation, a fear or hesitancy of allowing anyone else to get too close.

Cornell psychiatrist Dr. Helen Singer Kaplan writes of women who seek numerous lovers: ". . . most, in my experience, show signs of emotional isolation. For such women, promiscuous sexuality is a way of handling anxiety and depression."[31]

The solution for the one seeking sexual satisfaction is not to continue a series of shallow relationships but to work on developing one deep relationship, preferably with one's spouse. One study of the sex lives of over 40,000 men convinced the researchers that "happiness does not come from having lots of partners but from having good sex with the partner . . . [you] have."[32]

Still, though, it is impossible for any finite human being to meet all of one's needs. No one can provide total security, unselfish love, and close friendship 100 percent of the time, every minute of every day. To do that, one would have to be perfect. He or she would have to be all-powerful, all-loving, and all-knowing. In other words, he or she would have to be . . . God!

This is why we feel that, for anyone's marriage to be really complete and fulfilling, both partners need to include God in the picture. Frankly, this is the basis of our own love, commitment, and communication. We have found that, as we develop a close relationship with God and with each other, our needs are more than met. In fact, as the next chapter will show, He offers the vital dimension for a dynamic love and sex life!

CHAPTER ELEVEN

THE VITAL DIMENSION

A friend of ours quipped, "If God made love and sex, He can't be all bad." What we would like to propose in this chapter is that the God who designed love, sex, and marriage can be a significant factor in our total fulfillment.

The greatest aid to love, sex, and a strong relationship concerns relating to your partner as a total person. Human lives have three dimensions: 1) the physical (your body); 2) the mental (your mind—intellect, emotion, will); and 3) the spiritual (your spirit). In order to have a complete relationship it is important for a couple to relate on all three levels: body to body, mind to mind, spirit to spirit. If any level is missing, the relationship is incomplete.

One older student at a large southern university illustrated this graphically. (In his midforties, he had returned to school to get his degree.) After class he said:

My wife and I have been married for 25 years. We've had a physical relationship, somewhat of a mental relationship, but no spiritual relationship at all. I can see now that many of the problems of the last 25 years could have been avoided if we had related on all three levels.

The spiritual area is very often the vital dimension in a successful relationship. We explained to him the way to relate best on a spiritual level.

It all centers around the most unique Person of history, Jesus of Nazareth.

"Jesus? Do you mean Jesus as in 'Jesus Christ'?"

The same.*

"Oh, no! What could Jesus Christ possibly have to say about sex that could be good?"

Don't be alarmed. Contrary to what some people have thought, Jesus and the Bible have a lot of good things to say about love, sex, and marriage. In fact, Christ can make any couple's sex life better! Some people picture God as a mean, long-bearded ogre who looks down over the rim of heaven and shouts to us humans, "Hey! Are you having fun down there?" We sheepishly reply, "Well . . . (gulp) . . . yyyesss." Then God says, "Well, cut it out!" The God of the Bible is not like that at all. He is a God of love and is infinitely concerned with our well-being.

The biblical documents present a very positive view of sex and sexuality. Remember the spicy love songs we quoted earlier? They said things like—

Let her breasts satisfy you at all times;
Be exhilarated always with her love.[1]

and

His abdomen is carved ivory . . .
. . . His legs are pillars of alabaster . . .
. . . His mouth is full of sweetness.
And he is wholly desirable.

Do you know where we found those juicy verses? You guessed it: the Bible! One of the best sex manuals ever written is the Song of Solomon in the Bible.

Sex and Spirituality

Fortunately, more and more people are realizing that love, sex, marriage, and spirituality can mix well together. For exam-

---

*Note that the word "Christ" is an English rendition of a certain Greek word. That Greek word translates the Hebrew word "Messiah," or "Anointed One."

ple, in September of 1975, *Redbook* magazine published the results of a study of female sexuality. The study, conducted by a professional sociologist, involved 100,000 women and was called the most extensive since the Kinsey Report (of the late forties and early fifties). One of the things the researchers attempted to learn was whether a correlation exists between the intensity of a woman's religious convictions and her pleasure in sex. Based on the reports of the women themselves, they concluded that—

> *Sexual satisfaction is related significantly to religious belief.* With notable consistency, the greater the intensity of a woman's religious convictions, the likelier she is to be highly satisfied with the sexual pleasures of marriage.[3]

Startling, to say the least! A year later, *Redbook* conducted another survey to gather more information about women and their beliefs. This time 65,000 women participated, and in April 1977 the magazine published the results. In addition to the positive link between sexual pleasure and spiritual convictions, the study presented a surprising picture of the spiritually oriented female:

> The religious woman has never been a popular heroine in this country. In movies and books "churchgoing" is often a code word, preparing us to meet a woman who is tight-lipped, narrow-minded, stern and prudish. That image can now be discarded . . . . *Redbook*'s new religion survey . . . shows the religious woman to be optimistic, openhearted, generous, forgiving and independent. . . . The more religious a woman is, according to our survey, the happier she is. That's true both in the way she rates her happiness and in what she says about certain symptoms of sadness. The very religious woman, for example, is least likely to report frequent feelings of anxiety, tension or worthlessness. The "moderately religious" woman is more apt to have these negative emotions. They are commonest to the woman who says she is only "slightly religious."[4]

Of course we're not using these studies in an attempt to prove anything about the truth of religion or values. We merely cite them to draw attention to the fact that a large number of people today do associate strong spiritual beliefs with healthy love lives and pleasure in sex. If they've found something good, perhaps it is worth investigating.

Is it worth it to consider Jesus Christ if He can make your love life better? Or your life better? Not only did He claim to be God (and back up His claim with evidence),[5] but He also offers qualities that can affect everyone in a personal way, including the areas of love, sex, and marriage. This is His package deal: the ability to love, the strength to sustain a commitment, the freedom for clear communication, plus complete forgiveness and power to live successfully. Jesus put it this way: "I came that they [people] might have life, and might have it abundantly."[6]

New Life

Christ's entry into one's life enables that person to begin living with an added spiritual dimension and to have eternal life.[7] As one grows in his (her) relationship with Christ, his attitudes and actions become increasingly fulfilling. The maturing Christian experiences the most challenging and rewarding life possible.

Earlier we said that love, commitment, and communication were keys to developing a strong relationship and a fulfilling sex life. Here is how Jesus Christ relates to those qualities and how He can make your life better.

Love

Christ can give a person the ability to love another person with *agape* love. When you're all tied up in your own guilt, self-centeredness, or personal frustrations, it's often difficult to be concerned for others. Christ's forgiveness releases you from preoccupation with your own hangups and gives you the power to love yourself and to love others. It's not completely forgetting yourself, but a resolution of inner conflict, an increased self-acceptance, and a new inner strength that motivates you to love with God's love. That is what real, perfect *agape* love is—the unconditional love that God demonstrated by sending His Son to die for us.

A first-century Christian had this to say about God's love:

We need have no fear of someone who loves us perfectly [as God does]; his perfect love for us eliminates all dread of what he might do to us. . . . So you see, our love for him comes as a result of his loving us first.[8]

Another early believer wrote that it is God who gives us the power to love others with *agape*.[9] He also described some of the characteristics of unconditional love:

Love is very patient and kind, never jealous or envious, never boastful or proud, never haughty or selfish or rude. Love does not demand its own way. It is not irritable or touchy. It does not hold grudges and will hardly even notice when others do it wrong. It is never glad about injustice, but rejoices whenever truth wins out. If you love someone you will be loyal to him no matter what the cost. You will always believe in him, always expect the best of him, and always stand your ground in defending him.[10]

We ask you, what man or woman wouldn't respond to love like that from his or her mate? Of course none of us is perfect in loving others; we'll probably always have some conditions in our love. But Jesus gives us the power to love less conditionally.

Commitment

Christ also enables a couple to develop a closer commitment to each other. When partners have a growing relationship with Christ, they'll find an increased trust. This is not to say that they'll never make mistakes. We see bumper stickers from time to time that say, "Christians aren't perfect . . . just forgiven!" After we trust Christ we still commit sins. The difference is that we have Christ to forgive us and give us strength to improve. It is this fact that can strengthen a couple's trust and commitment in their relationship. If each knows that the other is closely linked with the same Leader, each can have a greater confidence that his (her) union is secure. They're both part of the same team.

Before marriage, Linda feared that she might someday lose the love of her potential mate. "The basis for working out this fear," she says, "lay in recognizing the kind of relationship that my husband had with God. His commitment to God and His principles is the foundation for his commitment to me."

Perhaps one reason that so many couples choose to live together rather than to marry is because they fear they cannot keep a commitment. Having the integrity to value commitments, they choose to avoid a commitment rather than make one and break it. The benefit of knowing Jesus Christ personally is that He not only sees us through the difficulties that can threaten a bond but also provides guidance in the initial selection of the best partner for us. Trial and error need not be a factor.

What if someone's partner has had premarital or extramarital sex or has failed his or her partner in some serious way? Does this mean that he (she) can never keep a commitment again, can never be trusted? As we've seen, premarital sex and extramarital sex can seriously affect the relationship. Nevertheless, trust can grow as the couple grows together over time. In a marriage in which each partner follows Christ, He can work supernaturally to erase fears, enhance forgiveness, and develop trust. Commitment to Jesus helps the growth of commitment to each other.

Communication

Christ also helps a couple communicate openly and honestly. On a spiritual level, He tunes them in to each other. On the mental and emotional level, He frees people to be vulnerable. Insecurity or fear of being hurt or rejected can cause one to crawl into a shell and hide. Most of us have experienced this, if not to a major degree, then to a minor one. We may be afraid to admit a fault for fear that the other person won't support us or won't understand us. But Christ gives us an eternal security; He loves and cares for us no matter what happens. One early Christian wrote:

> I am convinced that nothing can ever separate us from His love. Death can't, and life can't. The angels won't, and all the powers of hell cannot keep God's love away. Our fears for today, our worries about tomorrow, or where we are—high above the sky, or in the deepest ocean— nothing will ever be able to separate us from the love of

God demonstrated by our Lord Jesus Christ when He died
for us.[11]
That type of love and security frees a person to take risks in the
relationship, to be transparent, to admit his needs or
shortcomings, and to give without expecting anything in return.
Two partners with a working understanding of Christ's security
have a strong basis for becoming good communicators.

This increased communication can enhance the entire personality. Rusty says, "Several people have commented that I've
become more outgoing since I've been married. I believe that
much of my natural reserve has lessened because of the relaxed
atmosphere in our home. This relaxed atmosphere is a direct
result of our relationship with Jesus Christ."

Another key to good communication is a reliable and effective
third party. Linda says, "It's amazing how much wisdom and insight God gives me into my own life and Rusty's life. I'm convinced that I could never be successful in a marriage, and
specifically in relating to Rusty, without God's counsel."

Forgiveness

Jesus Christ offers forgiveness for every wrong we've ever
done. This forgiveness is important to a couple because it
fosters self-respect, an essential quality for any good relationship. No matter what mistake a person has made, God is willing
to forgive and forget. He can do this because Jesus has died on
the cross in our place, bearing the punishment we deserved.
"God loved the world so much that he gave his only son, so that
anyone who believes in him shall not perish, but have eternal
life."[12] One person dying for others. *That* is unconditional love!

Often people know about Jesus Christ and have heard that
He died for us, but they find it hard to understand what that
means on a personal level. "How could His death on the cross
nearly two thousand years ago have anything to do with our
lives today?" they wonder. Here is an illustration that may help
clarify the issue.

Imagine that you are a traffic judge and also a parent. Let's
say your son is caught speeding and is brought before your for
trial. You try him, find him guilty, and sentence him to a

100-dollar fine or 30 days in jail. Suppose he is broke and can't pay the fine. As a loving parent you might not want him to go to jail, but as a just judge you would have to send him to jail. What would you do?

There would be an alternative. You could pay the fine for him. You wouldn't have to, but you could if you wanted to. That is a picture of what God did when He sent Christ to die for us. He loved us but saw that we were separated from Him. Some psychologists call this separation "alienation." The Bible simply calls it "sin," meaning a condition of separation from God.

Because of sin, our access to God is blocked and our lives are not as fulfilling as they could be. If the plug of a floor lamp is pulled from the wall socket, contact with the electric current is broken and the light goes out. This is similar to our condition. We all exist initially as "unplugged" from God. Some of the more obvious manifestations of sin are murder, thievery, war, etc. Some of the least obvious are worry, anxiety, and lack of purpose of life (difficulties which, by the way, can greatly affect fulfillment).

One early follower of Jesus wrote that everyone has sinned and fallen short of God's perfect standard.[13] (That's not too hard to believe. If a university student tells us he's never sinned, we just ask his or her roommate! In a marriage, we ask the mate.) Christ's follower also said that the consequence of sin is spiritual separation from God.[14] Unless something had been done for us, we would have had to spend time and eternity in this "unplugged," unfulfilled state.

The Solution

Christ came to solve the problem. When He died physically on the cross, He made the *total payment* for our sins. He died spiritually as well, so that we could be forgiven. Just as you, the traffic judge, could choose to pay the fine for your guilty son, so God chose to pay the fine for us. "He *Himself* bore our sins in His body on the cross."[15] He took the rap for us. In other words, God took the sinless Christ and poured our sins upon Him. Then, in exchange, He poured God's goodness into us![16]

In the traffic court illustration, your son could refuse the

100-dollar fine if he wanted to, and choose to go to jail. It's the same with Christ. God loves us. He offers us complete, total forgiveness of all our sins—past, present, and future.[17] There are no strings attached. We don't have to promise anything. All we have to do is to believe that Christ died for us and to accept His forgiveness as a free gift.

Remember that at the end of the last chapter we said we would return to the question, "What if you've already been involved in premarital or extramarital sex?" Guilt can be a tremendous barrier to happiness in life. A person who has been involved in premarital or extramarital sex (or anything, for that matter) can be completely forgiven if he or she comes to Christ. Your mind can be cleansed of all past guilt. You don't have to walk around feeling down on yourself, burdened with condemnation. You are an important person: Jesus Christ died for you! He can remove that burden and give you a positive self-image. He can restore the freedom of love and trust in a relationship.

David was a king, a great leader of ancient Israel. He was also a man who made many mistakes. One time he committed adultery with the wife of one of his top soldiers who was off fighting a war. Then he arranged for the husband to be killed. "What a jerk!" you might say. You're probably right. Later, though, he realized that what he had done was wrong. God forgave him. Listen to what David writes about the joy of knowing he was forgiven:

High as the heavens are above the earth,
So great is His [God's] loving kindness toward those
   who revere Him.
As far as the east is from the west,
So far has He removed our transgressions from us.[18]
What happens for those whose guilt has been forgiven!
What joys when sins are covered over! What relief for
those who have confessed their sins and God has
cleared their record!
There was a time when I wouldn't admit what a sinner I
was. But my dishonesty made me miserable and filled
my days with frustration. All day and all night your
[God's] hand was on me. My strength evaporated like

water on a sunny day, until I finally admitted all my sins to you and stopped trying to hide them. I said to myself, "I will confess them to the Lord." And you forgave me! All my guilt is gone.[19]

A young woman at the University of Vermont wrote about her experience. "Having tried premarital sex, I can really understand the reason to wait. I regret having made the mistake (it *was* a mistake), but I thank God that He has forgiven me and given me back more than I lost of myself." No matter how great the sin, or how small, God stands ready to forgive.

Power

Jesus also offers a new spiritual life with power. This new power can greatly affect one's love life. One of the most common questions we get from people who have been involved in premarital sex or extramarital sex (or any other habit that is destructive to a relationship) is, "In the light of what you've said, I'd like to stop but I don't have the power." One student in California told us, "Your comments pertaining to sexuality, especially premarital sex, I find emotionally feasible but physically impossible." Another man in New England was more blunt: "How do you turn off the faucet?" One woman said, "I don't have the power to say no." Others say, "I'd never have the ability to keep the commitment that a marriage demands." But Christ can give you the strength.

Not only did He die for our sins, but He also rose physically from death to give new life. (The resurrection of Jesus Christ is one of the best atested facts of history.[20] We won't take time here to present the evidence, but we suggest that you investigate the references we've cited in this.) Jesus explained that everyone is born physically alive but spiritually dead (i.e., with a spiritual vacuum). In order to properly communicate on a spiritual level, we must be spiritually reborn. Spiritual rebirth can profoundly affect our sex life.

One evening a great religious leader named Nicodemus came to Jesus to talk. Nicodemus was so religious that he prayed seven times a day and went to synagogue three times a day. He tried to be perfect in everything he did. Jesus told him,

"Unless one is born again, he cannot see the kingdom of God."

As you might imagine, "Nic" was a bit shocked. "How can I be born again when I am old?" he asked. "Can I reenter my mother's womb and be born a second time?" Jesus went on to explain that He wasn't talking about a physical birth (which we all undergo) but a spiritual birth. All the good works (and in the case of Nicodemus, religious observances) in the world wouldn't get a person close to God. Nor does the good outweigh the bad. "You must be born again," Jesus said.[21] This happens when one accepts Christ's forgiveness by faith and asks Jesus to live in his life. Then that person will have a new inner power—the living Christ—in his or her life.

Jesus explained how a person can enter into a relationship with Him by faith. He said, "Behold, I stand at the door [of your heart or life] and knock; if anyone hears My voice and opens the door, I will come into him or her."[22] He stands at your life's door, seeking entrance. If someone were knocking at the door of your room, there would be three things you could do: ignore him and hope he'd go away, tell him to go away, or open the door and invite him in. It's the same with Christ: you can ignore Him, tell Him to get lost, or invite Him in.

Receiving Christ involves simply believing that He died for you, accepting the forgiveness He offers, and inviting the living Christ into your life. It's saying in faith, "Jesus Christ, I need You. Thanks for dying for me. I open the door of my life and receive You as my Savior (i.e., the One who died for my sins). Thank You for forgiving me. Give me the fulfilling life You promised."

The Personal Key

In an earlier chapter we said that many people who are approaching marriage wonder, "How can I become the right person?" We promised that we would return to that question. We believe that the key to becoming the right person is to get the right Person—Jesus Christ—inside you. Believing in Christ doesn't make you perfect in daily living. Rather, once you have met Him, He can work in your life to mature you and help you become all that you want to be. This doesn't mean that you'll become a robot or a puppet. Rather, you can become the person you were designed to be!

Jesus Christ can make a big difference in a marriage too. We view our own marriage as a triangle. God is at the top corner and Linda and I are at the bottom two. We find that, as we grow closer to God, we also grow closer to each other. Of course, there are rough spots along the way. But the fact that we're each following the same Leader makes those rough spots easier to handle. We find that, as we grow in faith, we each become freer to give ourselves unselfishly. *That* is what draws us closer together.

Does Jesus make a couple's life better? We're convinced that He does. Two marriage partners who have growing relationships with Christ will grow closer to each other: spirit to spirit, mind to mind, body to body. Their love, commitment, and communication will become increasingly dynamic. As one California woman put it, "Twenty-two years as a wife (and the last 8½ years as a Christian) enable me to agree with you 100 percent!"

Does all this make sense to you? Have you received Christ yourself? Do you know He lives in your life? You *can* know. He said, "If you open the door, *I will come in.*" Jesus Christ is no liar. You can take Him at His word and believe that if you ask Him to forgive you and enter your life, He will do just that. We're not talking about becoming a member of a church, joining an organization, or promising God that you'll live a perfect life. We're talking about accepting a free gift and inviting the living Christ to live in your life.

Many who have desired to receive Christ have expressed their faith through prayer. Prayer is simply talking with God. You can talk to Him in the quiet of your own heart. He is much more concerned about your attitude than your specific words. Below is a short prayer that many people have used in receiving Christ:

Lord Jesus, I need You. Thanks for dying for me. I open the door of my life and receive You as my Savior (the One who died for my sins). Thank You for forgiving me. Give me the fulfilling life that You promised.

Does that express the desire of your heart? If so, we encourage you to pray it (or something similar in your own words) right now, wherever you are, and Christ will come into your life as He promised.

Believing God

Did you ask Jesus to forgive you and enter your life? Did He do it? Of course He did (if you asked) because He said He would! He said, "If you open the door, *I will come in.*" So you can believe He is in your life right now if you asked Him in.

Don't worry if you don't feel different (or if you *do* feel different now but the feelings go away in a short time). The Christian life is lived by faith in God's trustworthiness and in His promises, not by feelings. Feelings can come and go. Sometimes they are a result of believing God by faith. At other times they reflect more the complexities of human personality than the work of God in one's life. The important thing to remember is that Jesus will never leave you once He has entered your life. He said "I will never desert you, nor will I ever forsake you"[23] and "I am with you always."[24] He gives you eternal life the moment you receive Him:

God has given us eternal life, and this life is in His Son.
He who has the Son has the life; he who does not have the
Son of God does not have the life. These things I have
written to you who believe in the name of the Son of God,
in order that you may know that you have eternal life.[25]

If you have just received Christ, we would like to send you some materials (at no cost to you) that will help you begin to grow in your faith. If you will drop us a postcard or letter at the address shown below, telling us you have made this decision, we'll be happy to get this information to you.

Our address is:
Rusty and Linda Wright
Arrowhead Springs
San Bernardino, CA 92414

CHAPTER TWELVE

INFINITE HELP

One of the major reasons that people finally give up on their marriage is that they have reached a state of hopelessness. They fear they can't change. They fear their partner can't change. Their marriage seems doomed. This is where the Christian life, if applied, can make a big difference.

God has provided help. But how do we practically apply that help in the complexities of love, sex, and marriage? Linda relates an experience of hers.

When I finally said "I do," I was shocked at how difficult the marital adjustments and problems were. For example, with almost everyone I meet, I'm cool and calm. I don't take their opinions or remarks so seriously that it disrupts my life. But with Rusty I wear my feelings on my sleeve.

It took awhile for me to determine why I overreacted and how to get control of the situation. Let me explain specifically how I went about it.

I talked with God. "Lord, I don't want to overreact, but the problem has the best of me. Could you help me understand why I overreact and how to control it? With that prayer (and I prayed it often) small bits of insight began to come to me. (I did better if

I wrote those insights down.)

As I began to understand the source of my overreaction (usually fear, guilt, or resentment), I asked God to deliver me from them. First I asked God to fill me with the Holy Spirit so I would experience His power in combating these deep-seated reactions. Then I read specifically about these areas in the Bible and memorized a few verses to help me remember.

Understanding

One of my best aids was to help Rusty understand what I had come to understand about myself. When he could see how and why I responded the way I did, it helped him watch his behavior toward me.

Rusty applied the Spirit-filled life by asking the Holy Spirit to fill him and help him be gentle and supportive of me. He memorized verses like "Where there are many words, transgression is unavoidable." For the most part, except when he is under pressure, he has developed sensitivity. (By the way, Linda develops the concept of how to change patterns of thinking and living in her book *Success Helper*.)

Rusty relates another incident. When we married, I wasn't in touch with my feelings very much. So I was not capable of understanding Linda's feelings very well. After I got a good look at my insensitivity, I became nervous about doing anything for fear I'd make a mistake. Linda remembers one night during my learning experience.

But Dogs Are Sensitive Too!

A small black dog showed up on our front steps one evening. He looked like a stray, so we took him in and fed him. That evening as I was preparing dinner, the dog kept coming into the kitchen bothering me. I asked Rusty if he would make the dog stay in the living room. Rusty would voice some feeble command for the dog to "sit" and "stay." But the dog would jump back up and head for the kitchen.

After several repeats of this, I began to get upset. I couldn't understand why Rusty couldn't do a simple thing like making a little dog mind. I took the dog aside and told him firmly to "stay." He did. So at last I turned to Rusty. "Rusty, why can't you make the dog behave?" I'll never forget the precious answer he gave.

"Linda, you know how you've been telling me about how things you do and say can affect people for the rest of their lives. And you've said that I need to understand how people feel and think so that I don't hurt them but help them. Well, what if I'm insensitive to this dog? What if I talk too strongly and ruin his life forever?"

Rusty continues: "I have often prayed for understanding of where people are and why. I sometimes drill Linda to find out what's behind her decisions, how she sees others, and why certain people behave as they do. The Holy Spirit has assisted me time and time again in urging me to observe and learn. When I become insensitive I admit to God that I am wrong; I ask Him to fill me again with His spirit and continue to help me develop in this area.

We said before that marriage was a relationship and not a system. Nor is it role models or pat answers. The beautiful part for the Christian in a marriage relationship is that we have a Helper, the Holy Spirit, to aid us in making the best decisions.

Here's an example of how this works. Let's say there is a legitimate financial crisis in a family—not an imagined one (because you can't afford a new TV), but a real one. The big question is, Should the wife work? Now if you ask one set of people they will say "Certainly." In fact, the woman will never be fulfilled unless she has a career. Not only *go* to work, but make it your *priority*. Another group would answer "Certainly not." A wife or mother should *never* work. You have just heard from the pat-answer crowd, the role-model experts.

But remember we said that marriage is a relationship—two distinct people in a unique relationship. That complicates things a little. When you throw out the "always" statements and the "marriage mold," you have to use your brain to come up with an acceptable solution for a particular situation.

Here's where a relationship with God makes a big difference. God knows each of us intimately. He knows what is best for us—what will hurt us and what will help us. As we seek Him He can give us the right solution *if* we are not already hemmed in too tightly by the "experts." You see, in the Christian life, each person can be his or her own expert under the leadership of the Lord. This does not mean that we do not seek counsel, for counsel is part of God's plan. However, we are not bound to current thinking, preconceived ideas, and pat answers.

Our faith affects our relationship in many ways. It gives us a source of internal strength, strength that enables us to display unselfish attitudes. (Please note that what follows may not make much sense to you if you have not yet received Christ. If you have not yet received Christ, we suggest that you do so before proceeding.)

God promised the power of the Holy Spirit to enable Christians to live more effectively. The Holy Spirit enters a person the moment he or she believes in Christ. He will never leave that person.[1] However, the Holy Spirit only empowers an individual as that person allows Him to. God promises all the power and love resources we need, when we need it. Our will is the switch that allows the power to become operative.

Spiritual Breathing

When we find ourselves becoming uptight, angry, anxious, etc., a simple biblical principle helps us return to a more positive mental attitude. The principle is sometimes referred to as "spiritual breathing." Physical breathing has two main aspects: exhaling and inhaling. You exhale the bad air and inhale the good air. Spiritual breathing has the same two parts.

Exhale: When we become aware of sin in our life (i.e., something that displeases God in our attitudes or actions), we simply admit to Him that we have sinned. This is called confession. To confess means "to say along with," to agree with God concerning our sin. We don't have to try to work up feelings of remorse or sorrow. We simply agree with God. A first-century Christian wrote, "If we confess our sins, He [God] is faithful and righteous to forgive us our sins and to cleanse us from unrighteousness."[2] We are forgiven all our sins the moment we receive Christ. However, confession of sins as we become aware of them helps make this forgiveness real in our experience. Exhaling can be thought of as "getting it off our chest" with God. We confess; He forgives and cleanses; then we can thank Him that we are forgiven and cleansed.

Inhale: Once we have confessed, we then ask God—in the Person of the Holy Spirit—to again empower our lives. Another term for "God empowering our lives" is "the filling of the Holy Spirit." When the wind fills the sail of a sailboat, it provides the power that the boat needs to move along the water. In a similar way, the Holy Spirit will fill (empower) our lives if we let Him. He will produce the "fruit of the spirit" (i.e., the results of being filled with the spirit). "The fruit of the Spirit of love, joy, peace, patience, kindness, goodness, faithfulness, gentleness, self-control."[3]

Be Filled with the Spirit

God *commands* Christians to be filled with the Spirit: "Do not get drunk with wine, for that is dissipation [waste], but be filled with the Spirit."[4] He also *promises* that if we ask Him something that is His will, He will answer: "This is the assurance we have in approaching God: that if we ask anything according to his will, he hears us. And if we know that he hears us—whatever we know that we have what we asked of him."[5]

We know that God wants us to be filled with the Spirit, for He commands it. So if we ask Him to fill us, He will do it. This is inhaling: asking God to fill us with the Holy Spirit and believing (based on His promise) that He has done it.

After hearing about spiritual breathing, one man said, "I understand how to breath spiritually now. My problem is that I'm afraid I'll be panting like a cat on a hot tin roof!" Certainly every Christian needs to breath spiritually often every day. However, as one grows in his (her) faith, he will find his attitudes and perspectives growing too. He will not become sinless but will sin less and less.

We should also caution against looking for immediate changes in *feelings* when one is breathing spiritually. This may happen, but most often the change is one of *attitude*. Emotions sometimes take awhile to catch up with our attitudes. We find that, as a problem comes in our relationship, we need to first be

sure our relationship with God is in order by breathing spiritually. Then it is often easier to work out our own point of discord.
(For more information on the Spirit-filled life, we recommend
the Transferable Concept series of booklets produced by Here's
Life Publishers, Arrowhead Springs, San Bernardino, California
92414.)

Talking with God

There are several other ways in which our faith affects our
marriage relationship. We find that prayer—talking with
God—provides a necessary channel. We can talk with God
about anything—our dreams, our job, our friends, our finances,
our sex life, each other. We try to pray together as much as
possible. Not only does this allow us to approach God as a
team, but it also helps us draw closer together.

Reading the Bible together continues to be a source of
encouragement and growth. The Bible is filled with practical
wisdom. Consider of few of these choice tidbits from the Book
of Proverbs:

A gentle answer turns away wrath,
But a harsh word stirs up anger.[6]

A man has joy in an apt answer,
And how delightful is a timely word![7]

He who restrains his words has knowledge,
And he who has a cool spirit is a man
    of understanding.[8]

When there are many words, transgression
    is unavoidable,
But he who restrains his lips is wise.[9]

The one who commits adultery with a woman
    is lacking sense;
He who would destroy Himself does it.
Wounds and disgrace he will find,
And his reproach will not be blotted out.

For jealousy enrages a man,
And he will not spare in the day of vengeance.
He will not accept any ransom,
Nor will he be content though you give him
      many gifts.[10]

The naive believes everything,
But the prudent man considers his steps.[11]

There is hope for any marriage. Maybe you are just starting out. Or maybe you have stacked up a series of disappointments and discouragements through the years. Regardless, there is hope.

If you are not a Christian, linking up to God through Jesus Christ is the best asset you will ever have for a successful marriage. If you are a Christian, availing yourself of the power of the Holy Spirit and the resources of God can bring about positive change.

CHAPTER THIRTEEN

CRUCIAL QUESTIONS

As you might suspect, lecturing in universities on such a controversial subject as love, sex, and marriage generates quite a bit of discussion. In this chapter we have included some of the questions that we have been asked as we travel, along with our answers or suggestions. Naturally, space will not allow us to deal with every possible ramification of love, sex, and marriage in this short book. Thus we've limited ourselves mainly to the most commonly asked questions. Nor do we pretend to know every answer to every question we are asked. We simply present the following material for your consideration.

What about premarital petting? How far should I go?

In a previous chapter we dealt with premarital intercourse. If a person disagrees with our views on this and chooses to go all the way before marriage, the issue of premarital petting has, of course, already been settled. One who chooses to wait until marriage for intercourse, however, still must decide how far to go. There is no clearly drawn line in the Bible regarding the specifics of petting. We could pick an arbitrary limit and state it, but if we did, it could be counterproductive. Different couples have different limits. Also, some would move immediately to the recommended limit and then ache with frustration.

One Christian marriage counselor explains some helpful principles regarding premarital affection that are drawn from the Bible. In his book *Solomon on Sex,* Joseph C. Dillow suggests that the bride in the Song of Solomon gives three bits of advice or warnings to singles. Rather than reproduce here his entire basis for this interpretation, we simply summarize his conclusions and refer you to his book (The numbers below refer to specific verses in the Song of Solomon).

2:7— Maximum joy and fulfillment in marital sex can be hindered greatly by allowing yourself to be premaritally aroused by anyone other than the one whom God intends for you.

3:5— Premarital sexual stimulation can greatly hamper objectivity in choosing your life's partner.

8:4— Dillow feels that this verse implies that premarital sexual involvement can be detrimental to postmarital sexual adjustment. He adds that this problem can be confirmed by any marriage counselor.[1]

Petting appears to be designed to culminate in intercourse. A small touch lights the fire, warm caresses fuel the flame, and heated passion grows into a mighty blaze. Premarital petting can be difficult to control. Simple hand holding is exciting at first, but that can soon lose its zing. Next comes the goodnight kiss. A while later there are wrestling matches in the parked car and more. The Law of Diminishing Returns sets in. Each new level of intimacy seems thrilling at first, but soon only a closer level brings excitement. Since intercourse is not the aim, the couple must stop somewhere, and that can be very frustrating.

The New Testament admonishes people not to "defraud"[2] others. Starting something you know you can't finish would seem to fall under that category. Know your point of no return, and if you're not sure what it is, stop sooner than you think you should. Hopefully, as the relationship deepens, there will be more freedom for open discussion of each partner's feelings on petting. If you feel your partner is more aggressive than you wish, be loving but firm. Clearly state your dislikes and limits. Avoid situations that can only be explosive.

Where should you fit among the various levels of premarital intimacy? At one extreme, holding hands is enough to start some people climbing the walls. At the other extreme, most would agree that fondling of the breasts, manipulation of the genitals, etc. help start something you can't finish. Your happy medium is probably somewhere in between. Even without knowing you, we'd recommend that you stick closer to the "holding hands" end of the scale (we did), simply because sexual excitation is such an emotionally explosive and potentially confusing factor. Remember, it's simple to blow out a match but very difficult to control a forest fire.

I still don't see what the big deal is about waiting for intercourse. Is it really such an earth-shattering experience? Why put up with extended frustration for a simple, pleasurable, biological/psychological experience?

This question was asked once by a senior at San Diego State who had just heard one of our lectures in his family studies class. Obviously, he found our reasoning unacceptable. We wonder, though, if his basic disagreement with us was not so much over logic as over different assumptions about the nature of sex. In fact, that may be the basis of many of the objections to biblical statements on sexual behavior. Many people feel that sex is merely "a simple, pleasurable, biological/psychological experience." One student in Pennsylvania noted, "Some animals mate for life and others don't. Shouldn't humans be able to make the same choice?" Another in California said, "I don't see what's wrong about having sexual intercourse just for pleasure" (i.e., with no emphasis at all on the relationship).

We feel that sex is more than "a simple, pleasurable, biological/psychological act." Sex is extremely complex and involves all that you are as a person. We get this view from the biblical documents. Moses, Jesus, and Paul all explained that when a couple enters into sexual intercourse, a unique relationship is established: the two become "one flesh."[3] This "one flesh" bond exists whether or not a strong interpersonal relationship exists.[4] It is difficult, if not impossible, to completely understand the meaning of this. The late C. S. Lewis, famous professor of Medieval and Renaissance Literature at Cambridge (and a one-time skeptic of Christianity) offered this insight:

> . . . the truth is that wherever a man lies with a woman,
> there, whether they like it or not, a transcendental relation
> is set up between them which must be eternally enjoyed or
> eternally endured."[5]

The "transcendental relation" that Lewis speaks of is perhaps the best perceived by the faint traces of emotional attachment or nostalgia that some say they have for various premarital partners. Interestingly enough, even the most seasoned (hardened?) sexual veterans, who deny any feelings for many of the people in their long string of sexual conquests, often have a twinge of emotion when reminded of "the first time." Possibly this too is at least partially a manifestation of the "one flesh" reality. Sex is special from the Christian perspective because it is a gift of God, and humans are made in the image or likeness of God.[6]

Naturally these views constitute a set of presuppositions—presuppositions that affect our views on sexual behavior. But the opposite view (sexual intercourse as a simple biological experience) is also a presupposition. As such, it also colors one's opinions on sexual matters. Everyone has a bias, and we have tried to clearly explain ours—that of biblical Christianity.

Note, however, that you don't have to believe in Christianity to hold many of these same views on sex. In fact, throughout this book we have attempted to include comments from a variety of secular researchers who support certain Christian stances without being Christians themselves. Masters and Johnson, David Reuben, and others certainly do not agree with every aspect of Christianity or with every facet of the biblical teachings on sex. Nevertheless, their views do coincide with a Christian perspective on a number of key points, as the cited references show.

What intelligent twentieth-century man or woman would base his or her life on such a superstitious fairy tale as Christianity? Everyone knows that Christianity is only a collection of myths.

To the contrary, there is a wealth of evidence to show that Christianity is true. The Christian does not need to take a blind leap of faith into the dark but can believe based on evidence. We all exercise faith every day. Few of us know everything about electricity or the laws of aerodynamics. Yet we have evidence of their validity: lamps and airplanes. Whenever we turn on an electric light or board an airplane, we are exercising faith—not blind faith, but faith based on evidence. The Christian does the same thing. There is plenty of evidence to support Christianity.

What kind of evidence? An in-depth survey would be beyond the scope of this book, but consider a few examples. The manuscript evidence for the New Testament alone, for example, is far superior to that of almost all other writings of antiquity, including those of Caesar, Plato, Tacitus, Thucydides, and Herodotus. Sir Frederic Kenyon, former director and principal librarian of the British Museum, was one of the leading authorities on the reliability of ancient manuscripts. Based on the evidence, he concluded, "Both the *authenticity* and the *general integrity* of the books of the New Testament may be regarded as finally established."[7]

The life, death, and resurrection of Jesus Christ comprise the cornerstone of Christianity. Jesus fulfilled over 300 Old Testament prophecies of the Messiah. These were written hundreds of years before He was born. One accurately foretold the place of His birth; another, the events of His death; a third predicted the exact day He would ride into Jerusalem on a donkey's back. A mathematician, Peter Stoner, once attempted to calculate the probability of just eight of the 300 prophecies being fulfilled in one person. He conservatively estimated that there was one chance in 10^{17} (1 in 100,000,000,000,000,000) that the eight predictions would come true in one person from the time they were written until the present. 10^{17} silver dollars would cover the state of Texas two feet deep, Stoner says. The chance that a blindfolded person could accurately pick a marked silver dollar from such a pile on the first try is one in 10^{17}. That's the same chance of the eight prophecies being fulfilled in one person by chance alone. You can read more about Stoner's findings in his book *Science Speaks.*[8]

The resurreciton of Jesus Christ is one of the best attested facts of history. He was executed on the cross and declared dead. His body was wrapped up like a mummy and placed in a tomb. A stone weighing several tons was rolled against the entrance. A unit of superior Roman soldiers was placed out front to guard against grave robbers. On the third day, the stone had been rolled away and the tomb was empty, but the grave clothes were still in place. The Roman guards came out with the feeble story that the disciples had stolen the body while they were sleeping. How could they know who had done it if they were asleep?

Meanwhile, hundreds of people were saying that they saw Jesus alive and were believing in Him because His prediction (that He would rise) had come true. Both the Romans and the Jewish religious authorities would have loved to produce the body to squelch the movement. No one did. Instead, Christianity spread like wildfire. The disciples, now convinced that Jesus had power over death, went on to die as martyrs as they boldly proclaimed their faith. Peter was crucified upside down. Thomas was skewered. John (according to tradition) was boiled in oil but survived, the only one to die a natural death. Each was confident that he had seen the risen Christ.[9]

One thing that made Jesus unique was that He claimed to be God. He said "I and the Father are one"[10] and "He who has seen Me has seen the Father."[11] Some people regard Jesus as simply a great moral teacher. C. S. Lewis, the one-time agnostic whom we quoted in the previous answer, had this to say about the possibility:

A man who was merely a man and said the sort of things Jesus said would not be a great moral teacher. He would either be a lunatic—on a level with the man who says he is a poached egg—or else he would be the Devil of Hell. You must make your choice. Either this man was, and is, the Son of God, or else a madman or something worse. You can shut Him up for a fool, you can spit at Him and kill Him as a demon; or you can fall at His feet and call Him Lord and God. But let us not come up with any patronizing nonsense about His being a great human teacher. He has not left that open to us. He did not intend to.[12]

Was Jesus a liar, a lunatic, or the Lord? From the evidence of His life and teachings, Lewis concluded that He was the Lord. We encourage you to investigate and decide for yourself. The Gospel of John (the fourth book in the New Testament) would be a good place to start. Four other helpful books (besides those in the Bible) are *Evidence That Demands a Verdict* and *More Than a Carpenter*, both by Josh McDowell; *History and Christianity*, by John Warwick Montgomery; and *Set Forth Your Case*, by Clark Pinnock.[13]

If there is so much evidence to support Christianity, why are there so many skeptics?

Probably many people are not aware of the evidence. But another major reason is that of guilt. Often people don't want to believe that Christianity is true because if it is true, it means that they are guilty. So they rationalize and convince themselves that it is false. Some who have engaged in premarital sex say they have felt no guilt and that the lasting effects are positive. It is often extremely difficult for people to admit (even to themselves) that they have committed a sin. Professor O.H. Mowrer, a psychologist at the University of Illinois (and *not* a professing Christian) points out the dilemma that many people face:

. . . human beings do not change radically until first they acknowledge their sins, but it is hard for one to make such an acknowledgement unless he has "already changed." In other words, the full realization of deep worthlessness is a severe ego "insult" and one must have a new source of strength to endure it.[14]

Jesus Christ provides that strength. He offers complete and total forgiveness. As an early Christian who once struggled with his own guilt finally saw, "There is now no condemnation awaiting those who belong to Christ Jesus. For the power of the life-giving Spirit—and this power is mine through Christ Jesus—has freed me from the vicious circle of sin and death."[15]

But why offer Christianity as a solution when it is the cause of so much guilt?

Some say that all guilt is socially conditioned, that if society didn't have moral codes, we wouldn't feel guilty. They say that guilt feelings come from past problems or from following outdated moral codes. Another view is that there is a Supreme Being who establishes what is right and wrong and tells us so because He loves us and knows what will fulfill us most. If the evidence supports this view (as we've concluded that it does), then the reason people feel guilty is usually because they *are* guilty. (We

say "usually" because there can be situations in which people experience false guilt.) If people don't feel guilty (or say they don't)
for doing something that this Supreme Being clearly says is
wrong, they are still guilty.

What we are saying is that it is not *Christianity* that makes
people guilty but rather *the people themselves.* Christianity offers a *solution* to guilt through faith in Christ. Of course, some
Christians have mistakenly promoted false ideas (such as "sex is
bad") that make people feel guilty. Such misrepresentations of
the biblical documents are wrong and should be opposed. But
God, as we've seen, is not down on the use of sex. He's down
on the *misuse* of sex.

Aren't morals relative?

Many people believe they are. "Do your own thing." "If it
feels good, do it, as long as it doesn't hurt anyone else." These
are common expressions of the philosophy of relativism. We
touched on this issue briefly when discussing the statistical and
cultural arguments for premarital sex.

Often people say, "There are no absolutes," yet they seem to
be absolutely sure of it! The statement "There are no absolutes"
is in itself an absolute statement. Besides this obvious incon-
sistency, relativism suffers from other major problems. If morals
are relative, who is to say what is right and what is wrong?
Where do values come from?

If morals are relative, can a person really say "If it feels good,
do it as long as it doesn't hurt anyone else?" When you add the
qualification "as long as it doesn't hurt anyone else" you have
made a value judgment. You have implied that it is bad or
wrong to hurt others. Suppose someone else (like a Hitler or an
Idi Amin) feels that it can be *good* to hurt others. If morals are
relative, who is to say that those two men were wrong?

"Those are bad examples," you say. "Everyone knows that
Hitler was wrong." Do they? A lot of Germans believed in him.
Even today there are vestiges of the Nazi party in the U.S. If
there is no Supreme Arbiter (i.e., God) to decide on moral
values, everyone decides for himself, and the consequences can
be disastrous. If there is a Supreme Arbiter to tell us what is right
and what is not, we can be freed from potential chaos and have

a basis for ethical action. This is why the existence of God and moral absolutes are important issues.

A real benefit of moral values in sex can be realized in the back seat of a parked car or in a private home or apartment or dormitory room late at night. When every urge and desire says "go ahead" and the Christian moral value says "stop," much future troubles can be averted. Having moral values can rescue us from those times when our reason is blurred by passion or obsession.

Don't knock premarital sex or extramarital sex if you haven't tried it.

One woman in New England said, "I really don't think you can put down premarital sex, never having experienced it." Then she added, "But I can't put down waiting since I can't experience it." It was almost as if she was beginning to see the fallacy of her own argument. To use experience alone as the basis for your behavior is a sham. Your own personal experience is not the only effective guideline for decisions in life. Reason, careful thought about the consequences, counsel with others, and (for the believer) counsel with God are all important.

When you stress the need for permanent commitment in marriage, you ignore the reality that people change. The commitment to the original person may be genuine, but later that person isn't the same anymore.

How true: people *do* change. That fact should motivate a couple to take a good deal of time getting to know each other and developing their interpersonal relationship *before* they agree to marry. Spending time together in a wide variety of situations—with each other's family and friends as well as alone—can be a help here.

In addition, the fact that people change should motivate us to seek divine guidance and wisdom in the choice of a mate. God loves us and knows who and what can please us the most, both now and in the long run. Looking back on our own decision to marry, and with all the uncertainties of twentieth-century life, we would have been very anxious about marrying each other if we hadn't sensed that God was in it.

What do you think about homosexuality?

"I have trouble relating to what you're saying," said one California student. "You're approaching all this from a straight perspective. I'm gay."

Our conclusions on this sensitive issue are drawn from careful research. Because of space limitations, our remarks on this will be brief. For additional information, we suggest that you consult the references we've cited.[16]

The most important biblical viewpoint of homosexuality is that a homosexual is a person for whom Jesus Christ died.[17] God loves us and wants only the best for us. He knows us better than we can ever know ourselves.[18] He knows what will fulfill us and what will hurt us. This is why He says that monogamous heterosexuality is best, that it is right. This is also why He says that homosexuality is wrong, that it is sin.[19] He knows that it won't fulfill us and that it can hurt us.

One problem with homosexuality is that the plumbing doesn't fit. Another is the potential difficulty to the family, a basic and foundational unit of society. Furthermore, it seems that brevity is characteristic of many homosexual relationships. As Dr. John White, counselor and professor of psychiatry at the University of Manitoba, writes, ". . . lifelong fidelity seems to be much more rare among homosexuals than among straights."[20]

Apparently a lot of homosexual relationships are not gratifying. Psychiatrist Lowen says:

> It is difficult for me to understand how the homosexual can be called "gay." True, homosexual parties and gatherings have a superficial appearance of carefreeness and lack of restraint. . . . [but] . . . The carefreeness and gaiety reflect the lack of strong feelings. They are masks that cover the inner deadness of the homosexual personality. On closer acquaintance and under analysis, the homosexual proves to be one of the most tragic figures of our times.[21]

Some have suggested that homosexual orientation and behavior result from physical differences in hormones, genes, and chromosomes. On this, Dr. White remarks:

> Science has so far searched vainly to find a physical basis for homosexuality. The testes of male homosexuals produce the same range of hormones as those of normal

men. The ovaries and other hormone-producing glands of homosexual women produce the same proportions of sex hormones as those of normal women.[22]

He goes on to say:

Scientific evidence seems to suggest that while our sex hormones may account (at least in part) for the fact that we exhibit sexual behavior and that we experience sexual urges, our sex hormones *do not necessarily determine either the kind of sexual behavior we indulge in or the sex of the person we choose as a partner.*[23]

Another writer, Bennett J. Sims, discusses the possibility of "constitutional" (i.e., genetically determined) homosexuality and offers this insight:

One wonders how much the insistence upon a "constitutional" homosexuality is not at bottom a contemporary expression as blaming God as a last resort, the shift of responsibility for one's being, and the parallel abdication of freedom. This is a very difficult question and needs to be dealt with compassionately even when conviction compels us to challenge the idea of "constitutional" homosexuality.[24]

"But," asked one young person, "suppose you've tried many heterosexual relationships, found none of them fulfilling, and then finally find happiness with a member of the same sex?"

God's knowledge of us and of our potential partner is infinite. He knows more about what contributes to a fulfilling and successful match than any number of trial runs could ever show us. And with all that infinite wisdom, he still recommends heterosexuality. Regardless of the level of happiness a person may *think* that he or she has reached, God says that He can make it better. It is certainly safer to trust the counsel of a wise and loving Creator than one's own limited sample of personal relationships.

If you are a homosexual, realize that God is not down on you as a person. He loves you and will give you complete forgiveness and a most fulfilling lifestyle if you'll let Him. As Sims writes, "In regard to homosexuality, the most important witness of Scripture is not condemnation, but the promise of liberation."[25]

I am a Christian and have problems with premarital sex. What should I do?

Any sin blocks our fellowship with God. We are completely forgiven the moment we receive Christ, but unless we are honest with God on a moment-by-moment basis, this forgiveness is not real in our lives. The Christian's response to sin in his or her life should be confession: "If we confess our sins, He is faithful and righteous to forgive us our sins and to cleanse us from all unrighteousness."[26] To confess our sins to God simply means to name them, to admit to Him that we've sinned. It doesn't have anything to do with promising to do better. We confess; God forgives and cleanses. Then, as we allow Him to control our lives by faith, the Holy Spirit gives us power to resist future temptation.[27]

Once you as a Christian have reopened lines of communication with God, there are several practical things you can do regarding premarital sex. You may need to ask forgiveness of someone you have wronged. Also, avoid frequenting secluded places that invite temptation. Instead, date in groups. Try praying together on a date. Some couples make a habit of praying at the start and end of a date. (Knowing that you'll close a date with a prayer can also serve as a check on your behavior as the evening wears on!) Others like to read the Bible together. The Psalmist wrote, "O magnify the Lord with me, and let us exalt His name together"[28]—certainly a fitting theme for any Christian relationship.

Be careful what you look at and what you read. Jesus said, "You have heard that it was said, 'You shall not commit adultery; but I say to you that everyone who looks on a woman to lust for her has committed adultery with her already in his heart."[29] For men and women, living involves the use of our minds as well as our actions.

If you find your desires becoming excessively strong, ask God for help. Meditate on appropriate portions of the Bible, such as those we've cited in the notes.[30] "Whatever is true, whatever is honorable, whatever is right, whatever is pure, whatever is lovely, whatever is of good repute, if there is any excellence and if anything be worthy of praise, let your mind dwell on these things."[31] Believe God and ask Him to prepare and guide you in the choice of a mate.

If I become a Christian, won't I lose all my freedom, especially in my sex life?

We are all slaves of something. Some people, even without realizing it, are slaves to their passions and are not as fulfilled as they could be. On the other hand, Christ offers tremendous freedom to those who follow Him. Here are some of the many freedoms available:

1) freedom to draw on Christ's resources and wisdom in every situation.

2) freedom to experience God's forgiveness.

3) freedom from anxiety, fear, and guilt about sex.

4) freedom from slavery to sex.

5) freedom from feeling the need to exploit sex in a relationship.

6) freedom to seek God's guidance on sexual questions.

7) freedom to relax in the presence of members of the opposite sex.

8) freedom from pressure to conform to the sexual attitudes, values, and actions of your peers.

9) freedom to forgive those who have hurt or used you.

10) freedom to accept yourself, to have a positive self-image based on God's love and acceptance rather than on others' evaluations of your worth, sexuality, etc.

11) freedom to trust God to lead you to your life's partner.

12) freedom to enjoy sex to the utmost, in its proper context.

Jesus Christ frees people to enjoy love, sex, and marriage to the utmost. He frees them to have self-respect. He said:

If you abide in My word . . . you shall know the truth, and the truth shall make you free. . . . If therefore the Son shall make you free, you shall be free indeed.[32]

Jesus can make you free indeed!

CHAPTER NOTES

Chapter 2
ALL YOU NEED IS LOVE

1. David Sunde, "How to Have a Three Dimensional Love-Life," in *Collegiate Challenge*, 1974, p. 9. Sunde cites George Sweeting, *And the Greatest of These* (Westwood, NJ: Fleming H. Revell Co., 1968), p. 39 (emphasis ours).
2. Interview of Dr. Elizabeth Kubler-Ross by Daniel Goleman, "The Child Will Always Be There: Real Love Doesn't Die," in *Psychology Today*, Sept. 1976, p. 56.
3. This illustration is adapted from Zig Ziglar, *See You at the Top* (Gretna, LA: Pelican Publishing Co., 1979), p. 46.

Chapter 3
HOW DO I LOVE YOU?

1. Proverbs 12:25.
2. Mark R. Littleton, "You Have Been Chosen to Clap and Cheer," in *Kindred Spirit*, Spring 1980, p. 4.
3. Ibid., p. 6.
4. Romans 12:10.

Chapter 5
WHY SEX?

1. David Reuben, M.D., *Everything You Always Wanted to Know About Sex But Were Afraid to Ask* (New York: Bantam Books, 1972), pp. 53-55.
2. Daniel G. Brown, Ph.D., "Female Orgasm and Sexual Inadequacy," in Ruth and Edward Brecher, eds., *An Analysis of Human Sexual Response* (New York: Signet, 1966), p. 129.
3. Proverbs 5:15-19.
4. Song of Solomon 5:10-16; 6:3.
5. Song of Solomon 7:1-9.
6. Song of Solomon 7:10-12.
7. Genesis 2:24.
8. William H. Masters and Virginia E. Johnson, *Human Sexual Inadequacy* (Boston: Little, Brown), 1970.

Chapter 6
GETTING THE MOST OUT OF SEX

1. William H. Masters and Virginia E. Johnson, *The Pleasure Bond* (New York: Bantam Books, 1976), pp. 113-14.
2. Theodore Issac Rubin, "On Relating," in *Mainliner*, Feb. 1977, p. 27.
3. Fred Belliveau and Lin Richter, *Understanding Human Sexual Inadequacy* (New York: Bantam Books, 1975), p. 74.
4. William H. Masters and Virginia E. Johnson, "Counseling with Sexually Incompatible Marriage Partners," in Ruth and Edward Brecher, eds., *An Analysis of Human Sexual Response* (New York: Signet, 1966), p. 207.
5. Joanne Koch and Lew Koch, "The Urgent Drive to Make Good Marriages Better," in *Psychology Today,* Sept. 1976, p. 34.
6. Reuben, op. cit., p. 25.
7. Ibid., p. 123.
8. Ibid., p. 158.
9. Alexander Lowen, M.D., *Love and Orgasm* (New York: Macmillan Publishing Co., 1975), p. 219.
10. Reuben, op. cit., p. 144.
11. Belliveau and Richter, op cit., pp. 81-82.
12. Lowen, op. cit., p. 191.
13. Masters and Johnson, *The Pleasure Bond,* p. 285.
14. Daniel G. Brown, Ph.D., "Female Orgasm and Sexual Inadequacy," in Ruth and Edward Brecher, op. cit., p. 163.
15. Reuben, op. cit., p. 76.
16. Gloria Steinem, "Is There Sex After Sex Roles?" in *Ms.,* Nov. 1976, p. 47.

Chapter 7
THE CART BEFORE THE HORSE?

1. Robert R. Bell, *Premarital Sex in a Changing Society* (Englewood Cliffs, NJ: Prentice Hall, Inc., 1966), p. 150.
2. Robert J. Levin, "The Redbook Report on Premarital and Extramarital Sex: The End of the Double Standard?" in *Redbook*, Oct. 1975, p. 40.
3. Many of the categories and names for these arguments are taken from Jon Buell, "Why Wait Till Marriage?" (lecture outline), and Jim Williams, "The Case for Premarital Chastity" (cassette tape), both produced by Probe Ministries International, 12011 Coit Road, Suite 107, Dallas, TX 75230.
4. Herbert J. Miles, *Sexual Understanding Before Marriage* (Grand Rapids: Zondervan, 1973), p. 91.
5. Masters and Johnson, *The Pleasure Bond,* p. 200.
6. Reuben, op. cit., p. 244.
7. Miles, op. cit., pp. 83-84.

8. Arnold W. Green, *Sociology, An Analysis of Life in Modern Society* (McGraw Hill Book Company, 4th ed., 1964), pp. 389-90, cited in Miles, op. cit., p. 83.

9. Green op. cit., pp. 404-05, quoted in Miles, op. cit., p. 84.

10. Green, op. cit., p. 39, quoted in Miles, op. cit., p. 109.

11. J. D. Unwin, *Sex and Culture* (Oxford, England: Oxford University Press, 1934), cited and quoted in Evelyn Millis Duvall, Ph.D., *Why Wait Till Marriage?* (New York: Association Press, 1970), p. 113.

12. Masters and Johnson, op. cit., pp. 34-35; see also Reuben, op. cit., p. 131.

13. Povl W. Toussieng, M.D., personal communication dated Oct. 8, 1964, quoted in Duvall, op. cit., p. 75.

14. Bell, op. cit., p. 78.

15. Miles, op. cit., p. 107.

16. Duvall, op. cit., p. 50.

17. Alexander Lowen, M.D., *Love and Orgasm,* (New York: Macmillan Publishing Co., 1975), p. 310 (emphasis his).

18. Paul Popenoe, ed., *Family Life,* Nov.-Dec. 1975, p. 5 (emphasis ours).

19. *Christianity Today,* Nov. 5, 1976, p. 86.

20. Reuben, op. cit., pp. 30-31.

21. "The War Against Disease: Many Gains—But Setbacks, Too," in *U.S. News & World Report,* Dec. 20, 1976, pp. 43-46.

22. Ibid.

23. Ursula Vils, "Preparing Teen-Agers Who Can't Wait," in *Los Angeles Times,* Mar. 21, 1976, Section V, pp. 1, 18.

24. Proverbs 17:27.

25. Lowen, op. cit., pp. 317-18.

26. William S. Banowsky, *It's a Playboy World* (Old Tappan, NJ: Fleming H. Revell), 1973, pp. 46-49.

27. Aldous Huxley, *Ends and Means* (1937), pp. 312, 315, 316, quoted in Buell, op. cit., p. 2.

28. Carol Tavris, "Men and Women Report Their Views on Masculinity," in *Psychology Today,* Jan. 1977, pp. 34-37 ff.

29. Ibid.

30. James Hassett, "A New Look at Living Together," in *Psychology Today,* Dec. 1977, pp. 82-83.

31. Masters and Johnson, *The Pleasure Bond,* pp. 191-92.

32. Tim and Beverly LaHaye, *The Act of Marriage* (Grand Rapids: Zondervan, 1976); Herbert J. Miles, Ph.D. *Sexual Happiness in Marriage* (Grand Rapids: Zondervan, 1974); Ed Wheat, M.D., & Gaye Wheat, *Intended for Pleasure* (Old Tappan, NJ: Fleming H. Revell, 1977).

33. "Premarital Experience No Help in Sexual Adjustment After Marriage," in *Family Life,* May 1972, pp. 1-2.

34. Paul Popenoe, Sc.D., personal interview, Los Angeles, CA, June 28, 1976.

35. Reuben, op. cit., pp. 137-39.
36. Duvall, op. cit., p. 53 (emphasis hers).
37. *Family Life,* May 1972, pp. 1-2.
38. Paul Popenoe, Sc.D., "Sex Aspects of Marriage," in American Institute of Family Relations (Los Angeles, n.d.), publication #14, p. 1.
39. Cited in Duvall, op. cit., p. 42 (the words are Duvall's).
40. Fred Belliveau and Lin Richter, *Understanding Human Sexual Inadequacy* (New York: Bantam Books, 1975), pp. 81-82.
41. Dwight Hervey Small, *Design for Christian Marriage* (Old Tappan, NJ: Fleming H. Revell Co., 1972), p. 246.
42. Robert O. Blood, Jr., *Marriage,* 2nd ed. (New York: Free Press, 1969), quoted in "The Fradulent New Morality," in *Family Life,* Oct. 1972, p. 2.
43. 1 Corinthians 6:18 KJV.
44. 1 Thessalonians 4:3 KJV.

Chapter 8
THE TIE THAT DOESN'T BIND

1. "Sinfully Together," in *Time,* July 9, 1979, p. 55.
2. Eleanor D. Mackline, "Going Very Steady," in *Psychology Today,* Nov. 1974, pp. 53-58; James Hassett, "A New Look at Living Together," in *Psychology Today,* Dec. 1977, p. 83.
3. "The Marriage Tax," in *McCall's,* Mar. 1978, p. 93; Forrest J. Boyd, "Observations," in *Decision,* Dec. 1979, p. 12.
4. Charles and Bonnie Remsberg, "The Case Against Living Together," in *Seventeen,* Nov. 1977, p. 132.
5. Ibid.
6. Ibid.
7. Ibid, p. 133.
8. Robert N. Whitehurst, "Living Together Unmarried: Some Trends and Speculation," unpublished manuscript (Windsor, Ontario: University of Windsor, 1973), pp. 11,12, cited in Carl Danziger, *Unmarried Heterosexual Cohabitation* (San Francisco: R & E Research Associates, Inc., 1978), p. 80.
9. Michael P. Johnson, "Commitment: A Conceptual Structure and Empirical Application," in *The Sociological Quarterly* 14:3, Summer 1973, pp. 401ff; David Walcott Beaudry, Ph.d., "Cohabitation and Marriage: A Comparison of Associated Communication Styles," in *Dissertation Abstracts International* 38:8, Feb. 1978, 3865-B.
10. Norman M. Lobsenz, "Living Together: A New Fangled Tango or an Old Fashioned Waltz?" in *Redbook,* June 1974, p. 186.
11. Eric K. Goldman, "How to Set Your Sweet Lover's Mind at Rest . . ." in *McCall's,* Mar. 1978, p. 86.
12. Christine Musello, "To Have and to Hold From This Day. . . to the Next," in *Ms.,* Nov. 1977, p. 57.

13. James L. Morrison and Scott Anderson, "College Student Cohabitation," in *The Education Digest* 39:9, May 1974, p. 59.
14. Karen Durbin, "Premarital Divorce," in *Harper's Magazine*, May 1974, p. 8.
15. See the previous chapter.
16. Musello, loc. cit.
17. Masters and Johnson, *The Pleasure Bond*, pp. 176-78.
18. Dr. Joyce Brothers, "Living Together Without Marriage," in *Good Housekeeping*, Jan. 1973, p. 51.
19. Nick Stinnett, et. al., *The Family and Alternative Life Styles* (Chicago: Nelson Hall, 1978), pp. 97,100.
20. Remsberg, op. cit. p. 162.
21. Richard R. Clayton and Harwin L. Voss, "Shacking Up: Cohabitation in the 1970s" in *Journal of Marriage and the Family* 32:2, May 1977, pp. 275-77.
22. Stinnett, et. al., op cit. pp. 92,93.
23. Ibid., p. 93.
24. Tim Stafford, " 'Living Together'—Experiment in Failure," in *Campus Life,* May 1978.
25. Eliezer Berkovits, *Crisis and Faith* (Sanhedrin Press), quoted in "Without Benefit of Clergy—Or Commitment," in *Christianity Today,* Mar. 4, 1977, pp. 32,33.
26. Ephesians 5:21-25.
27. Matthew 19.5.
28. John 10:10; Ephesians 5:18; Galatians 5:22, 23.

Chapter 9
REAL HARMONY

1. Ephesians 5:21 NIV.
2. Hebrews 10:24.
3. Ecclesiastes 4:9,10.
4. Proverbs 15:22.

Chapter 10
TRUE AND HAPPY

1. Marcia Lasswell and Norman Lobsenz, "Why Some Marriages Can Survive an Affair and Others Can't," in *McCall's,* Nov. 1977, p. 50.
2. Davidyne Mayleas, "Adultery: Should it Wreck Your Marriage?" in *Harper's Bazaar,"* Jan. 1980, p. 97.
3. "A Sex Survey: Most Women Admitted They Cheated on Husbands," in *The Miami Herald,* July 31, 1980, p. 15-A.
4. Marcia Lasswell and Norman Lobsenz, "What Being Faithful Really Means," in *McCall's,* Apr. 1979, p. 60.
5. Ibid.

6. "My Husband was Unfaithful," in *Good Housekeeping,* Feb. 1977, p. 36.
7. Ibid.
8. Ibid., p. 38.
9. Frederic F. Flach, M.D., *A New Marriage, A New Life* (McGraw-Hill, 1978), excerpted in "The Case for Fidelity," in *Good Housekeeping,* May 1978, pp. 139, 202.
10. Marabel Morgan, *Total Joy* (Old Tappan, NJ: Fleming H. Revell Co., 1976), excerpted in *Good Housekeeping,* Nov. 1976, p. 166.
11. Joyce Maynard, "How To Live with the 'Other Man' Fantasy," in *Ladies' Home Journal,* June 1979, p. 77.
12. Masters and Johnson, *The Pleasure Bond,* pp. 186-203.
13. Ibid., pp. 199-200.
14. Ibid., p. 203.
15. Ibid., p. 196.
16. Ibid., p. 197.
17. Ibid., p. 203.
18. Ibid., p. 176.
19. Ibid., pp. 176-78.
20. Ibid., p. 185.
21. Ibid.
22. "Act II: Sexually 'Open' Marriages Aren't So Hot After All," in *Human Behavior,* Oct. 1978, p. 48.
23. Nena O'Neill, *The Marriage Premise* (New York: M. Evans & Co., Inc., 1977), p. 112.
24. Ibid.
25. Ibid., pp. 200, 199.
26. Dr. Helen Singer Kaplan, "One Lover or Many?" in *Harper's Bazaar,* Mar. 1975, pp. 79, 118.
27. Shirley Streshinsky, "Healing a Hurt Marriage," in *Ladies' Home Journal,* May 1979, p. 64.
28. O'Neill, op. cit., pp. 54-55.
29. Ibid., p. 199.
30. Flach, op. cit., p. 202.
32. Kaplan, op. cit., p. 118.
33. Carol Tavris, "The Sex Lives of Happy Men," in *Redbook,* Mar. 1978, p. 109.

Chapter 11
THE VITAL DIMENSION

1. Proverbs 5:19.
2. Song of Solomon 5:14-16.
3. Robert J. Levin and Amy Levin, "Sexual Pleasure: The Surprising Preferences of 100,000 Women," in *Redbook*, Apr. 1975, p. 52 (emphasis theirs).
4. Claire Safran, "65,000 Women Reveal How Religion Affects Health, Happiness, Sex, and Politics," in *Redbook,* Apr. 1977, pp. 127, 217.

5. Josh McDowell, *Evidence That Demands a Verdict* (San Bernardino, CA: Campus Crusade for Christ, 1972), pp. 81-273.
6. John 10:10.
7. 1 John 5:11-13.
8. 1 John 4:18, 19 TLB.
9. Galatians 5:22,23.
10. 1 Corinthians 13:4-7 TLB.
11. Romans 8:38,39 TLB.
12. John 3:16 TLB.
13. Romans 3:23.
14. Romans 6:23.
15. 1 Peter 2:24.
16. 2 Corinthians 5:21 TLB.
17. Colossians 1:14; 2:13,14.
18. Psalm 103:11,12.
19. Psalm 32:1-5 TLB.
20. McDowell, op. cit.; Clark H. Pinnock, *Set Forth Your Case* (Nutley, NJ: The Craig Press, 1967); J. N. D. Anderson, *The Evidence for the Resurrection* (Chicago: InterVarsity Press, 1968); John Warwick Montgomery, *History and Christianity* (Downers Groves, IL: InterVarsity Press, 1964).
21. John 3:1-8.
22. Revelation 3:20 paraphrased.
23. Hebrews 13:5.
24. Matthew 28:20.
25. 1 John 5:11-13.

Chapter 12
INFINITE HELP

1. Hebrews 13:5.
2. 1 John 1:9.
3. Galatians 5:22,23.
4. Ephesians 5:18.
5. 1 John 5:14,15 NIV.
6. Proverbs 15:1.
7. Proverbs 15:23.
8. Proverbs 17:27.
9. Proverbs 10:19.
10. Proverbs 6:32-35.
11. Proverbs 14:15.

Chapter 13
CRUCIAL QUESTIONS

1. Joseph C. Dillow, *Solomon on Sex* (Nashville: Thomas Nelson Inc., 1977), pp. 139-40. (See also pp. 32-34, 39-40, 50-51 ff.)

2. 1 Corinthians 6:8; 1 Thessalonians 4:6.
3. Genesis 2:24; Matthew 19:5,6; 1 Corinthians 6:16.
4. 1 Corinthians 6:16.
5. C. S. Lewis, *The Screwtape Letters* (Macmillan, 1941), p. 93, quoted in M. N. Beck, "The Bed Undefiled," *Christianity Today,* Oct. 10, 1975, p. 5.
6. Genesis 1:27.
7. Frederic G. Kenyon, *The Bible and Archaeology* (New York and London: Harper, 1940), pp. 288-89; quoted in John Warwick Montgomery, *History and Christianity, His* magazine reprint, Dec. 1964-Mar. 1965, p. 6 (emphasis is Kenyon's).
8. Peter W. Stoner, *Science Speaks* (Chicago: Moody Press, 1969), pp. 99-108 ff.
9. See Josh McDowell, *Evidence That Demands a Verdict,* pp. 185-273, for a much more thorough documentation of resurrection evidences.
10. John 10:30.
11. John 14:9.
12. C. S. Lewis, *Mere Christianity* (New York: The Macmillan Company, 1972), p. 41.
13. McDowell, op. cit.; McDowell, *More Than a Carpenter,* (Wheaton, IL: Tyndale House Publishers, 1977); John Warwick Montgomery, *History and Christianity;* Clark H. Pinnock, *Set Forth Your Case* (Nutley, NJ: The Craig Press, 1968).
14. O. H. Mowrer, "Sin, The Lesser of Two Evils," in *The American Psychologist* XV:5 (May 1960), p. 301, quoted in Henry R. Brandt, Ph.D., *The Struggle for Peace* (Wheaton, IL: Victor Books, 1974), pp. 17-18.
15. Romans 8:1,2 TLB.
16. See Alexander M. Lowen, M.D., *Love and Orgasm* (New York: Macmillan Publishing Company, 1975); Kent Philpott, *The Third Sex?* (Watchung, NJ: Logos, 1975); Kent Philpott, *The Gay Theology* (Plainfield, NJ: Logos, 1977); Bennett J. Sims, "Sex and Homosexuality," in *Christianity Today,* Feb. 24, 1978, pp. 23-30; John White, *Eros Defiled* (Downers Grove, IL: InterVarsity Press, 1977).
17. John 3:16.
18. Romans 11:33-36.
19. Leviticus 18:22; 20:13; Romans 1:26,27; 1 Corinthians 6:9-11.
20. White, op. cit., p. 112.
21. Lowen, op. cit., p. 75.
22. White, op. cit., p. 116.
23. Ibid. (emphasis his).
24. Sims, op. cit., pp. 27-28.
25. Ibid. p. 27.
26. 1 John 1:9.
27. Ephesians 5:18; 1 John 5:14,15; Galatians 5:22,23; Acts 1:8.
28. Psalm 34:3.

29. Matthew 5:27,28.
30. 1 John 2:5-17; 1 Peter 2:11; Psalm 23; Psalm 119:9-11; Philippians 4:13,19.
31. Philippians 4:8.
32. John 8:31,32,36.